CW00351127

The Art of the Harley

3

4

First published in 1998 by Booth-Clibborn Editions,
12 Percy Street, London, W1P 9FB
in association with Barbican Art Gallery
on the occasion of the exhibition *The Art of the Harley*
22 January – 26 April 1998.

Distributed world-wide and direct mail through:
Internos Books
12 Percy Street
London W1P 9FB

info@internos.co.uk
www.booth-clibborn-editions.co.uk

Exhibition:

Selected by Tim Remus and Conrad Bodman
Organised by Conrad Bodman
Designed by Urban Salon
Graphics by Windpower

Catalogue:

Edited by Conrad Bodman
Designed by Society, London
Colour Reproduction by Dot Gradations Ltd. UK.
Printed and bound in Italy

The Art of the Harley

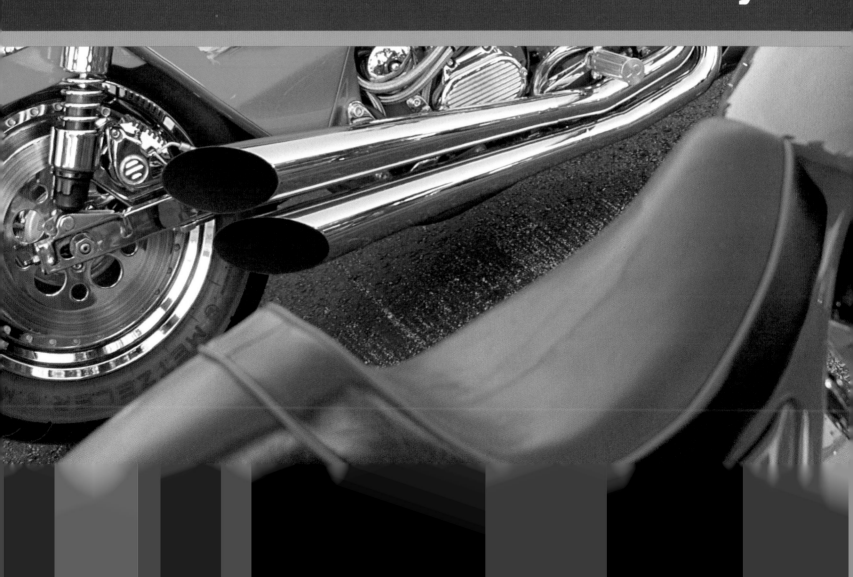

FLIGHT DEVIL

CHOKE

Contents

8 *Flight DeVille*
by Tank Ewsichek

9

10 Day turns to night, Daytona
Bike Week, Florida

Foreword

When asked to suggest what is particular to America, we could all start compiling a list of characteristics, geographical features, products and activities that seem especially American, and this list would inevitably get bigger and bigger. Remember: everything's BIG in America, or so it seems from this European viewpoint.

When the Gallery staff were invited to devise a programme of exhibitions for an American festival at the Barbican Centre, our list of desiderata got bigger and longer, until we asked ourselves what was uniquely American; what revealed the inner core of the country's character, when constructed as an exhibition. With the globalisation of culture that has advanced in the last fifty years, it becomes harder to identify elements that can still be attributed to a particular country, untainted by outside influences. With art exhibitions, the revealment of international cultural influences, which dilute and modify uniquely native characteristics, is an inevitable consequence of any study that tackles part of a melting-pot like America.

Yet, a chance exchange between my colleague Carol Brown and me, when thinking about the things most quintessentially American, put me on the trail of an extraordinary subject. Harley-Davidson is now the only major motorcycle manufacturer remaining in the United States, and an exhibition devoted to the art of customising its machines encapsulates everything that can be seen to be uniquely American in its flamboyance and style, as well as its allegiance to a name and product that is time-honoured and lasting.

The Art of the Harley is an exhibition unlike any that I have commissioned before. While it has a forerunner in a display called *Bike Art*, which Michael Diamond's team produced for the Gas Hall, Birmingham, from which we drew inspiration, this exhibition has, because of its uniqueness, attracted more 'Wows!' in advance of its launch than any other display that I have seen at Barbican Art Gallery. When I showed images of Arlen Ness' *Ferrari Bike* or *Two Bad* to unsuspecting audiences, the reaction was instantly ecstatic, but no-one questioned whether we would be creating a 'real' art exhibition, one that sheds perceptive light upon a cultural phenomenon grounded in identity, desire for freedom and individuality as well as belonging.

The diversity of the project's appeal, its supercharged brashness and its outrageousness in suggesting that the process of customising motorbikes can be elevated to that of an art form have all convinced observers that *The Art of the Harley* is unique.

It would not have been possible to realise this exhibition without support from many quarters. In particular, special thanks go to Willie G. Davidson and his colleagues at Harley-Davidson in Milwaukee, including Steven J. Piehl and Dr. Marty Rosenblum; as well as David Taylor, Jeremy Pick and Roy Pinto at Harley-Davidson (UK) Ltd. Our sponsor John Warr has been a real enthusiast and I would like to thank him and the staff of Warrs Harley-Davidson, London for their help and encouragement.

Tim Remus, whose books introduced me to the wonders of Harley custom building, has been a leading light in this project and has

selected the American bikes in the exhibition. Conrad Bodman (Exhibition Organiser) has steered the show to its successful realisation and joins me in thanking the following individuals who have assisted in the development of the project in the UK: Peter Alcock, Rikki Battistini, Jeff Duval and Rick James at Battistinis Custom Cycles, Dave Batchelar (P&D), Robin Bradley, John Carroll, Bill Gradley (Harley Trading Post), Maz Harris, Anne Parisio, Martin D. Pinner (JWR), Peter Ray, Garry Stuart and our advisors – Tony Dowden, Ian Mutch, Paul Parslow and Snob.

We would like to thank the following people in Europe who have assisted with the selection of European custom Harleys: Pascal Driessen, Frankie (Frankie's Parts, Sweden), Rainer Grasberge (Zweirad-Museum, Neckarsulm, Germany), Ulf Jensen (Harley-Davidson Club Sweden), Reinhold Paukner (Paukis Harley-Davidson), Horst Rösler (*High Performance* magazine, Germany), Paul Timpson (Zodiac International UK).

Many people in the USA have assisted in the creation of this exhibition. They include: Tim Remus (Exhibition Selector), Jim Betlach (Drag Specialties), Nace Panzica (Custom Chrome), Bobby and Arla Sullivan (Sullivan Brothers).

Our thanks go to all of the builders of custom Harleys for contributing to this project. In the USA: Dave Bell, Rick Doss, Bob Dron, Don Hotop, Cyril Huze, Bob McKay, Arlen Ness and family, Dave Perewitz and Tank Ewsichek; in the UK: Battistinis Custom Cycles, Steve Morley, Jeff Murphy (Riverside Cycles), Andy Peters, George Savage, Richard Taylor; and in Europe: Nicolas Chauvin, DiDi (Custom Ranch), Danny Franssen, Kenth Arvidsson and Marié Rashussen.

Finally our thanks go to the following owners who have lent works to the exhibition: Jill Bell, Flicks, Billy F. Gibbons, Mark George, Martin Henderson (Boot Hill Motorcycles), Bobby and Arla Sullivan, Vintage Magazine Company, Zweirad-Museum, Neckarsulm, Germany and to all of the lenders who wish to remain anonymous.

John Hoole
Curator
Barbican Art Gallery

11 John Hoole riding *The FXR-SS* by Battistinis Custom Cycles

12 Contest for best male tattoo at early
1980s British Tattoo Convention

Ted Polhemus

The Customised World

Our age is characterised by an extreme and remarkable juxtaposition of opposites. On the one hand, a delight in conformity – a herd instinct which finds comfort in labels (be they those of Calvin Klein, Reebok or Harley-Davidson). On the other hand, a hunger for unique individuality which inclines us to value the customised (be it a motorbike, a car, a tattoo, a painted black leather jacket, a distinctively DIY-ed home, a non-packaged holiday or an unusual hairstyle).

Either way, we are what we consume. That is, we are known to others by our choice of products and/or by the way we modify and use those products. Objects (including our own bodies) have become a kind of language – one which we employ to advertise 'where we are at'. (Or, more likely, where we would like to be at, or indeed where we would like to be seen to be at.) This reverses a previous arrangement whereby we were identified by our role in production rather than consumption: one was a tinker, a tailor or a candlestick maker, one was working, middle or upper class, etc. Today you are the sort of person who wears Calvin Klein (including a T-shirt which

makes this fact explicit), who drives a Ford Sierra, who eats at Harvester restaurants, who drinks Bacardi Breezers, who goes on holiday in the Algarve, who listens to the Pet Shop Boys and who subscribes to *Which?* magazine. Or, you are the sort of person who wears a patched denim jacket with a T-shirt which reads 'Fuck Off', has 'Live to Ride' tattooed on your arm, drives a customised Harley with apehanger bars and shorty pipes, who eats egg, chips and beans in greasy spoon cafes, who spends every summer travelling to custom bike shows, who listens to Pink Floyd and who gets *Back Street Heroes* magazine. (Or, you could situate yourself at an infinite number of intermediate points: for example, a Calvin Klein-wearing, Ford Sierra-driving, Harvester-eating, Bacardi Breezer-drinking, *Which?*-reading guy who has bought a 'factory-customised' FXSTC Softail custom Harley which he rides to custom bike shows when not on holiday in the Algarve.)

Whatever the products, whatever their message, the common ground is their value as visual communication. The use of objects to 'say' something – to signify – is hardly unique to our times. Indeed, it is as old as our species (the feather headdress which

13 Biker at Kent Custom Bike Show, Britain, 1997

14 'Live to Ride' petrol tank cap cover

15 Harley-Davidson '88 FXSTC Softail
© Harley-Davidson

indicated rank, the designs painted on a mud hut which indicated one's clan, the carved motifs on a spear which indicated tribal membership, etc.). What does, however, distinguish our contemporary use of objects as communication is our extraordinary range of choice – of objects, styles and, of course, messages. Previously, while the type of feathers used in a headdress, the colours used to decorate your mud hut, the particular motifs carved onto your spear and so on were tightly restricted by one's cultural tradition, now we are virtually uninhibited in our selection. Today, we can have it all. All at once if we so choose. We live in an amazing supermarket of style where you can have the Fiat Punto with or without the sunroof, the Big Mac with or without the onion, the Reebok trainers with or without the air-pumped cushion soles.

And yet, at the same time, the objects with which we surround ourselves, which we buy and which we use to signal personal identity, have never been so standardised – so mass-produced to an identical likeness of each other, so targeted in their marketing and advertising to specific 'lifestyle' types. It is this paradox (on the one hand our free-

dom of choice, on the other hand our mass-marketed consumption) which has given rise to both the possibility and the desirability of customising.

Customising could not and would not exist without mass production. There must be the standard, factory-produced model before there can be that messing around with the norm to produce the unusual variant. Never creation from scratch, always variation on an established, industrially-produced theme, customising was both made possible and made desirable by the advent of mass production.

Most of human history has been characterised by that hand-crafted, personal production of objects which can now be found only in those few (ever declining) tribal and peasant cultures which preserve traditional ways of life. In such a world there is no such thing as customising since there is no standard model to individualise. Consider the case of the 'Iceman' whose body and personal effects were discovered frozen in the Alps a few years ago. Some 5,200 years old, the Iceman lived at a time when every object was a unique product of handcraftsmanship and nothing was 'off the peg' or mass-

16 Harley-Davidson VR1000 racing

© Harley-Davidson

Rocker at '59 Club party,
London 1994

Since the Iceman's day, human history has seen a gradual standardisation of products. Two events, however, dramatically accelerated the rate of this process: the Industrial Revolution and Henry Ford's invention of assembly line production. Not only did these events create the possibility of mass-produced, virtually identical products, but in centralising manufacturing they created national (and then global) products which undermined regional distinctiveness. Perhaps even more importantly, such products could be mass-marketed and advertised – in the process graphically realising as never before an image of Mr and Mrs Average who bought the same products in the same packaging and lived out their lives with the same expectations and dreams as everyone else. The advent of television in the 1940s – and more significantly, its popular spread in the 1950s – brought the process of standardisation to its logical conclusion.

It simultaneously revved up the drive towards customisation. In other words, it is surely no coincidence that the era which saw the flowering of customising – of bikes, cars, clothing, body adornment, the home and 'alternative culture' in the fullest sense – was also the era which saw the fully developed and televised effects of mass production coupled with mass marketing. Nor is it a coincidence that the customising renaissance was most vividly seen in America which, more than any other country at the time, led the way in the creation of a fully standardised and blandly homogenised society.

Growing up in suburban America in the 1950s, I saw this transformation at first hand: the huge housing developments which overnight replicated a few 'model homes' (split level, ranch, Cape Cod) into infinity; the magazines like *Life* which (in advertising and editorially) projected a vision of strictly defined, happy normality in weekly instalments; that standardisation of design which in any given year made one car look more or less like another, one stereo a clone of

produced. His cloak of woven grass, his leather stockings and loincloth, his tattoos, his shoes of leather and straw, his dagger, his tassel with its ornamental stone bead, his arrows and quiver, even his bronze axe would all have been made as unique, one-off creations. If another Iceman was found from the same time and the same village his artefacts might be similar but none would be identical.

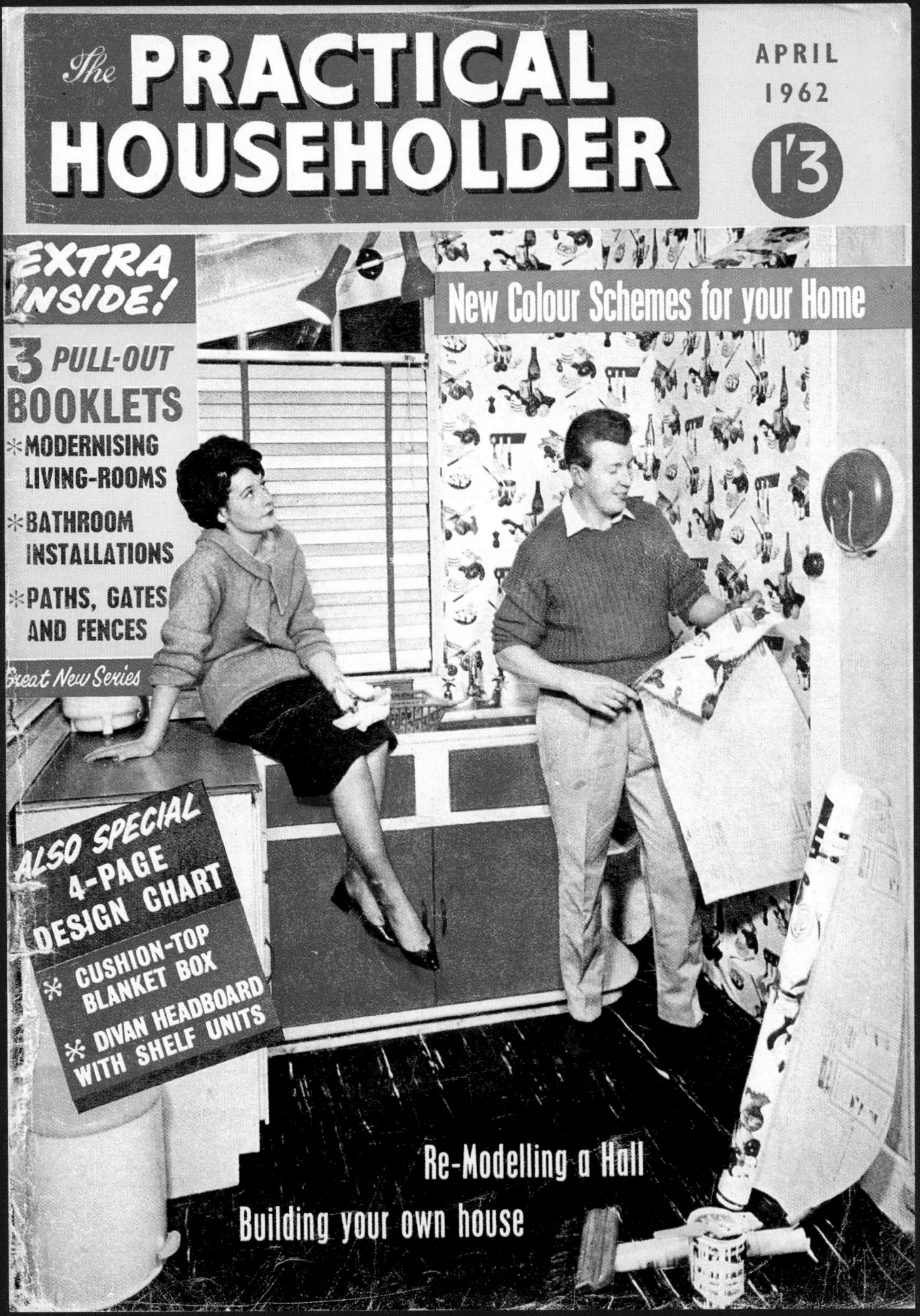

The PRACTICAL HOUSEHOLDER
APRIL 1962
1'3
EXTRA INSIDE!
3 PULL-OUT BOOKLETS
*MODERNISING LIVING-ROOMS
*BATHROOM INSTALLATIONS
*PATHS, GATES AND FENCES
Great New Series
New Colour Schemes for your Home
ALSO SPECIAL 4-PAGE DESIGN CHART
* CUSHION-TOP BLANKET BOX
* DIVAN HEADBOARD WITH SHELF UNITS
Re-Modelling a Hall
Building your own house

18 *Practical Householder* magazine

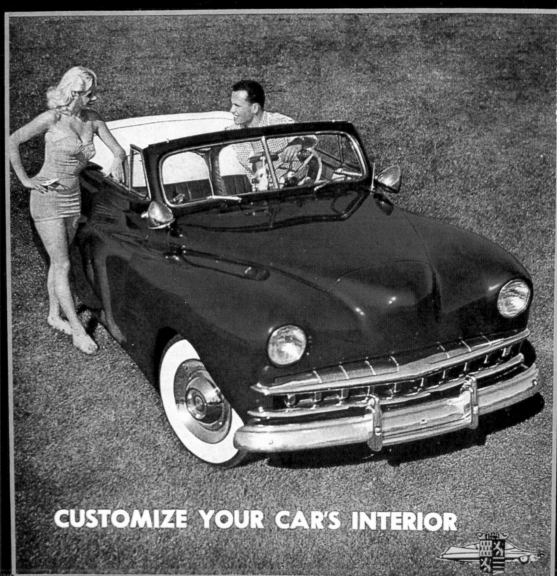

MOTOR TREND

The Magazine for a Motoring World

JULY 1951 25c

TESTING THE NEW ECONOMY CHAMP
by Griff Borgeson

The Rebuilt Engine Racket

CUSTOMIZE YOUR CAR'S INTERIOR

Shirley's *Ultra-Bird*, a 1958 custom T-Bird

The Dragon by Ralph Fisher

A swap meet at Sturgis

odds with mainstream society. 'What you rebelling against, Johnny?' – 'What you got?' Lenny Bruce or Gerry Mulligan, Jack Kerouac or Neal Cassidy, any of the motor-cyclists who stormed Hollister California and inspired *The Wild One*, those sun-bleached 'beach bums' who waited for the perfect wave at Big Sur or sought it out in Hawaii, and Elvis, Jerry Lee or Carl Perkins shaking all over in their blue suede shoes were all – each in their own, distinctive way – trying to find an escape from that undifferentiated mass which America had become.

This rebellion from the norm was expressed in customised clothing and adorn-ment styles (painted black leather jackets, distinctively patched denim, long hair, unusual jewellery, tattoos), in music (rock & roll, modern jazz, folk, country & western) and, where possible, in the form of customised motorcycles or automobiles. Less radically (but not, I think, without significance), Mr and Mrs Average tried to escape their standardised fate by custom-

another; and, finally, the coming of TV which left all of (white, middle class) America laughing at the same jokes and aspiring to the same way of life (complete with the same patio furniture, the same barbecue and the same leisurewear).

Needless to say, the stupefying sameness generated an opposite reaction. Hipsters, Beats, Bikers, Surfers and Rockabillies all occupied alternative cultures radically at

ising their homes with their own DIY experiments. The more homogenised and normal America became, the more its citizens strove to customise themselves, their homes, cars, motorbikes and possessions. (Until, of course, customising itself would be institutionalised 'as standard' – a subject we will return to in conclusion.)

And where America led, the rest of the world followed, with customisation riding the crest of the wave of standardisation as it washed over Britain, Europe and Australia – the prospect of a stifling futuristic uniformity (think of those '50s sci-fi movies where everyone is dressed in identical catsuits) triggering a hunger for individuality and a means with which to express it. In another age, this hunger for the unique would have generated an expansion of creative craftsmanship with artisans producing more idiosyncratic, one-off products (as in, for example, the Italian Renaissance). We, however, have chosen another course: to deconstruct, reconstruct, invert, subvert and

23 Back tattoo, British Tattoo Convention, early 1980s

24

25 Customised clothes and unique 'tats' on show at the Kent Custom Bike Show, 1997

Tattoos, piercings and jackets worn at Harley rallies in the UK and USA

play with the very standardised, mass-produced products which threaten to drown us in a sea of sameness. Thus was born the uniquely post-industrial, post-modern customised world – a place where the extraordinary is always defined, derived, referenced and measured from the baseline of the ordinary.

While the urge to be 'different' was shared by all those who felt stifled by mass production and marketing, its effects differed markedly depending upon individual circumstances. For the middle class family, satisfaction would have to be derived from using the ever-expanding ranges of DIY products to convert a standard 'box' into a unique home with plenty of 'character'; transforming the identical into the distinctive. As an editorial in *Do It Yourself* magazine put it: 'If you are not yet a do-it-yourself fan why not make a start now? In an age of sameness it provides a unique outlet for your own creative impulse, a chance to air your own good taste.'*

Typically, that customising of the home which drove the DIY revolution way beyond the practical necessity which initially spawned it was directed by a purely feminine aesthetic – the wife being the traditional (and now literal) 'homemaker'. Even if hubby did most of the manual work he would inevitably defer to his wife's 'taste'. (Realising this, the manufacturers of DIY products such as paints, wallpapers and fittings aimed their advertisements at women rather than men.) Cars and bikes, on the other hand, remained a typically masculine domain and their customising (as with tattooing, the only body adornment traditionally defined as 'masculine' in the West) expressed a male rather than a female aesthetic.

Furthermore, DIY wasn't a viable option of personal expression for those who rented rather than owned their homes. Thus (while there were certainly exceptions) the customised home became a primarily middle class and feminine art form, and the customised car or bike became a medium of

working class and male artistic expression. Furthermore, while the former was typically an expression of married life with couples working as a team, the latter reflected the lifestyle of single people – especially young males. Unhindered by mortgages, children, a settled career and a need for professional respectability, such independent individuals could carry their rebellion further – transforming their vehicles, themselves, their attitudes and lifestyles into something far, far removed from the prescribed normality of modern life.

Both DIY 'home improvement' and car/bike customising began as economic and practical necessities and then eventually became mediums of aesthetic expression. But as well as having differing demographic profiles (of income, home ownership, marital status, etc.), they also flourished within differing organisational structures. While home DIY came to be an amateur activity defiantly cut off from those professions which had traditionally been entrusted with it (with paints and other DIY materials specifically developed and marketed for go-it-alone amateurs), those involved with car or bike customising were very often professionals whose income came from car and bike repair or maintenance – their activities revolving around a workshop where tools and skills could be shared and where male-to-male bonding could occur outside the increasingly tight boundaries of the nuclear family.

Thus, whereas DIY was carried out within the home (each nuclear family having its own workshop in the cellar or garage), the customising of cars and bikes in workshops often provided a focus outside the home – a place of male-to-male interaction, teaching and learning. As such, a parallel could be drawn with that other centre of male-dominated customising: the tattoo parlour. Significantly, both of these institutions are based upon a system of apprenticeship whereby technical skills and aesthetic innovations are passed on from one 'generation' to the next by means of direct,

37 National Chopper Club badge and tattoo proudly displayed at British Tattoo Convention, Dunstable, Britain, mid 1980s

38 Harley-Davidson tattoo and belt buckle on show at the Kent Custom Bike Show, Britain, 1997

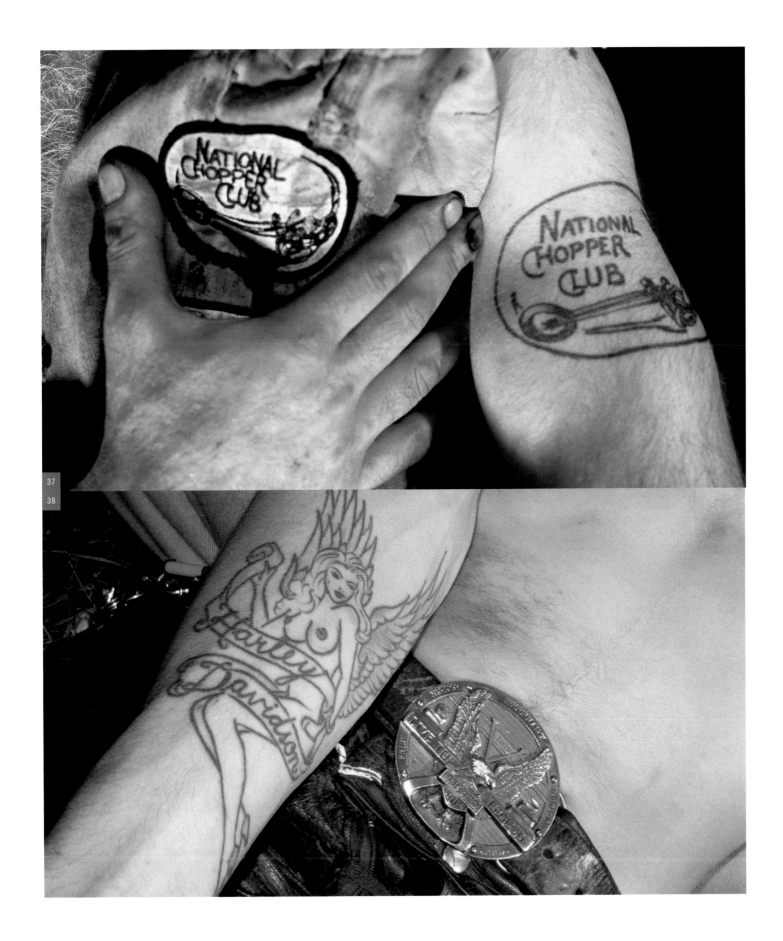

more creative pursuits, so too more and more tattoo parlours in the West became centres of artistic experimentation. While previously a customer would simply point to a standard 'flash' design (identical copies of which could be found in tattoo parlours across America, Britain, Europe and Australia) and the tattooist would replicate it on the customer's skin as closely to the original as possible, the 'Tattoo Renaissance' which began in the West Coast of America in the 1950s produced a new breed of tattooist determined to provide each customer with a unique design. Once as standardised a product as Coca-Cola or a Chevy pickup (you could get exactly the same 'bluebird' tattoo in Plymouth, England or San Diego, USA), tattoos rapidly became an expression of individual difference.

In the process, many tattooists (for example, Cliff Raven, Ed Hardy, Bob Roberts, Leo Zulueta, Jamie Summers and Vyvyn Lazonga) became artists rather than simply technically proficient craftsmen/women – their products (I would argue) as valid an art form as a painting which hangs in a gallery. Which is not, of course, to say that all are 'good art'. But surely we cannot categorically exclude tattooing from the territory of art simply because it uses living flesh as its canvas. Surely too (it seems to me), the same could be said of many customised cars and bikes. It will be argued that their practicality – the fact that, unlike a Rembrandt or a Warhol, they actually do something; namely take you from A to B – automatically defines them as craft rather than art objects. Perhaps, but what of the fact that extreme customising may hinder or even destroy the functionality of a car or bike as a trans-portation vehicle? What of the fact that some 'show' cars or bikes have never actually been ridden in or on? Andy Peters' custom Harley, for example, has never been started.

Or, to look at this point from the other direction, what of the fact that Marcel Duchamp's famous 'ready-mades' (the bicycle wheel, the bottle rack, the urinal)

personal contact. An extremely ancient arrangement, this same apprenticeship system would have provided the Iceman with both his tattoos and his bronze axe.

At odds with, and nearly destroyed by, the less personal assembly lines of modern factory production and mass education, it was these surviving pockets of pre-industrial apprenticeship which became the focus of male rebellion against an ever greater regimentation, standardisation and homogenisation of 'normal life'. Just as more and more car and bike workshops switched from repair and maintenance to

Harley rider with shoulder tattoo
© Harley-Davidson

could perform perfectly 'practical' functions if they had not been plucked from the real world to be exhibited as art? Bickering about the definition of art could lead us down a very dry, dusty and boring road. What is important is simply that we recognise the creative vision and skill which is so often to be found within the various customising communities. It shouldn't, of course, be necessary to say this. It should simply be obvious to one and all. But, as was once the case with graffiti art and is still very much the case with tattoo art, the working class backgrounds of car and bike customisers have tended to inhibit respect for their creations amongst the (still strongly upper

40 Andy Peters presents
    Eleganté, a radical super-
    charged Harley based on a
    1930s car design

41 Harley riders outside a diner
    © Harley-Davidson

class) 'Art World'. Happily, events like this exhibition of customised Harley-Davidson motorbikes at the prestigious Barbican Art Gallery suggest that such inhibitions and prejudices may be more typical of the past than of the future.

Yet at the very time when customising is attracting more broadly based respect, it is threatened as never before from within the automotive and motorcycle industries. What began as rebellion against mass-produced and mass-marketed standardisation has been institutionalised – consumed by the very beast it sought to slay. We have come full circle – with bike and car manufacturers now producing specialised lines which are pre-customised before they ever reach the consumer. Consider, for example, Mazda's 'MX-5 Le Mans 24' or Harley-Davidson's FXS Lowrider. In each such case, a unique, one-off, customised product has been replicated and sold in the manner of a 'limited edition'. As with 'narrowcasting' on television (making programmes for a particular target audience as opposed to broadcasting to an undifferentiated mass) the 'factory-customised' product addresses that diversity, heterogeneity and fragmentation which is the post-modern condition. In this sense – in finally rejecting modernism's fiction of a single yellow brick road of 'progress' upon

which we would all, as one, march into the future – the original customisers' rejection of mass conformism would appear to have triumphed. Our hunger for products with which to express our personal differences has been recognised. The individual, it could be argued, has triumphed over the mass.

Or, worryingly, has that spirit of individualism which fostered and empowered customising been itself mass-marketed – co-opted by its natural enemy? Personally I'm inclined to this latter, more cynical view. But it's not the end of the world – the customised world. Only the foolish have been fooled. Anyone with any sense can see that to clone the customised is to render the unique standard rather than the other way round. And meanwhile, in workshops and private garages throughout the world, the true customisers go on with turning the mundane into the extraordinary, the common into the special, the mass-produced into the unique – like medieval alchemists, transforming base metals into pure gold.

With thanks to: Giannino Malossi, Maurille de Smallem

*[as quoted in BBC's 1997 series *All Mod Cons*]

42 Mazda's 1991 Le Mans winner

43 Mazda MX-5 *Le Mans 24* limited edition

44 *Twin Blower* by Richard Taylor (detail)

45 A regular sight – Uncle Sam rides a
    Harley '45 and heads the Bike week
    annual parade at Daytona, 1994

Tim Remus

The American Custom Motorcycle

In the Beginning

Some motorcycle historians would trace the current craze for all things Harley-Davidson to the 'chopper' days of 1969 or '70, when every kid on every corner wanted a hog with a long springer fork. Yet, choppers evolved from earlier motorcycles, bikes that were often fitted with the same equipment made popular in the '70s.

The Second World War gave the sale of two-wheelers a big push as young GIs came home and bought motorcycles – often the same bikes they saw during their time in Europe. Thus many of the bikes on the streets during the 1950s and '60s were not Harley-Davidsons, but Triumphs, BSAs and Royal Enfields.

Many of those early Triumphs were 'customised' with a smaller petrol tank, a smaller seat and a Bates headlight. The idea was to simplify the bikes, eliminate anything that wasn't necessary, and replace the necessary things like handlebars with parts that had more style.

The Harley guys were doing very similar things to their bikes. Even before the war, riders were installing the longest of the factory front ends, though no-one was changing the fork angle at the time. After the war there were the beginnings of an aftermarket – at least there was somewhere to buy parts besides the local dealer. One of those 'new' stores, Flanders in Pasadena, California, offered an extensive line of accessories, including higher, narrower bars and the triple trees and parts needed to adapt them to then-current Harleys.

46   Petrol tank of *Santa Fe* by Dave Bell

47   Bob Dron aboard his early '70s chopper

B.C. – Before Choppers

The new handlebars went higher and higher and before long the riders were nearly standing up to reach the handle grips. It didn't take a brain surgeon to realise that these same riders looked like apes hanging from a tree. Names and slang terms like 'ape-hangers' evolved on the street and became part of the two-wheeled culture.

At the other end of the bike, a 'sissy bar' gave the passenger something to lean against, a backrest if you will. Sissy bars, combined with either apehangers or pull-back bars, helped to define the custom bikes being built in the late 1960s and early 1970s. Open any early 'chopper' magazine from that period and what you find are modified bikes built for the road – bikes that established a look and style that remains popular to this day. Harley riders started with a 74 cubic inch, essentially a full size Knuckle or Panhead, and stripped off anything that wasn't essential. Hardtail frames were the order of the day. Up front, a long, extended 'glide' or springer fork supported a twenty-one-inch front wheel.

Riders sat low on the bike with the legs stretched out to reach the 'forward controls' or 'highway pegs'. A contoured seat provided support for the back and helped the rider become part of the machine. Harleys were considered the best of this breed, though plenty of Triumphs and Hondas were modified in much the same way.

48 Larry Davis' chopper, built by Bob Munroe, 1968

49 Chopper built to commission by Bob Dron, 1971

50 Bob McKay's *Bar Hopper*

51 Chopper by Ken Schultz,
Sturgis, 1994

Choppers and the Aftermarket

The construction of all these bikes kept the early manufacturers busy and their advertising dollars helped establish the American motorcycle press. By the late '60s and early '70s, motorcyclists of the day had a number of magazines to choose from, each one filled with parts to buy and articles explaining how to correctly install them. Those early magazines carried ads for sissy bars, handlebars and custom seats. The list of available parts was quite extensive and included complete Hardtail frames, extended tubes for 'glide' forks, springer fork assemblies and a hundred smaller items.

Though anyone could bolt together a nice bike with the new parts, certain individuals began to develop a reputation for building complete bikes constructed from hand-fabricated parts. Among the feature bikes in the early magazines, certain names began to appear with regularity. Men like Arlen Ness, Dave Perewitz and Donnie Smith established themselves as professional custom builders – men who made their living building and selling custom bikes and fabricated parts.

52 Arlen Ness

53 *Flamed Chopper* by Arlen Ness
(detail)

The Motorcycle Press

The history of early customising is well documented by the early magazines. *Street Chopper, Chopper, Big Bike, Modern Cycle, Supercycle* and *Easyriders* began to cover the best of the bikes and carried ads from a hundred companies both large and small.

A water-stained copy of *Street Chopper* from 1970 carries ads for King and Queen seats manufactured by AEE, one of the first big suppliers of aftermarket parts. The same issue features a chopper from San Bernardino, California equipped with all the right stuff, including 'a special homemade springer (fork)…This thirty inches over stock springer was fabricated from chrome moly tubing… twenty-one-inch front wheel assembly with custom spool hub teamed with a 3.00X21 Avon Speedmaster tyre…' This same bike features a blue metalflake paint job and a 'Sissy bar that sweeps up and away from ribbed and bobbed custom fender which covers the 4.00X16 tyre and completely plated hub and brake assembly'.

Easy Rider

If one thing, one event, immortalised 'the look' of a long stretched-out motorcycle, it was the movie *Easy Rider*. Peter Fonda's bike set the pattern that is still being followed by builders and manufacturers today: Rake the frame and extend the forks to push the twenty-one-inch front wheel way out ahead of the bike. Design the seat to put the rider down low, add forward controls and a sissy bar. Keep the overall height of the bike low. Finish with plenty of chrome and a bright paint job.

Easy Rider captured the look, the spirit, that riders and builders had been working towards for twenty years. Tom Rudd, founder of the well-known aftermarket company Drag Specialties, remembers the movie well. 'The day after that movie opened the phone never stopped ringing. Suddenly everybody wanted a bike like the ones in the movie.'

Since that time, various motorcycle fads have come and gone, but the popularity of the American custom motorcycle refuses to go away. Testimony to the staying power of the look is as close as your favourite motor-cycle magazine. Check out the styling of the newest cruisers from Japan. Their look and lines can be traced directly to those early choppers and cruisers of '69, '70 and later. Open a copy of any current custom motor-cycle magazine. Retro choppers are all the rage, right down to the springer forks and Panhead engines. Even customs that don't copy exactly the earlier look owe much of their long, low look to those long stretched-out haulers of yesteryear.

54 Replica of the *Captain America* bike as ridden by Peter Fonda in the film *Easy Rider*

55 Rat bike (built from scrap parts) on the beach, Daytona Bike Week, Florida

The chopper phenomenon ran like a freight train all through the '70s. Big, Fatbob tanks went in the junk heap, replaced by smaller Sportster and Mustang tanks moulded into the frame. Front ends got longer and longer. At first it was Knuckle and Panheads, then Sportsters and finally Panheads and Shovelheads that got 'the chop'. Nobody left the bikes alone. Stock Harleys were in fact a canvas upon which each rider drew his or her own image. The riders did much of their own work and bought their parts at the local 'chopper shop'. Some of those chopper shops were actually fairly sophisticated paint and fabrication facilities run by men working to establish themselves as custom bike builders.

Factory Customs

Eventually the freight train of choppers running nose-to-tail down America's highways and byways did run out of gas. By the early 1980s, a series of events brought about the near extinction of choppers and custom bikes. One by one, the chopper shops closed or evolved into service facilities.

Part of the reason for this change was the soft American economy at the time, part

of it was the downturn in all types of motorcycle sales, and part of it was the fact that by 1980 you could buy a 'factory custom' from Harley-Davidson complete with extended forks, more rake, a twenty-one-inch front wheel, padded sissy bar and a red-on-black flamed paint job.

The flamed Harley-Davidson Wide Glide from 1980 was only the first in a long line of 'custom' bikes built at the Harley-Davidson factory. After years of ignoring the styles and trends on main street, those same styles began to show up on the new bikes from Milwaukee. Ad copy for the Wide Glide called it a 'California Classic', referring apparently to the birthplace of the design.

From Wide Glides, the factory quickly moved to the new Softail series of bikes. Based on a rear suspension design that Harley bought from an individual customiser, the new chassis put the rear shocks and springs under the frame. By using a triangulated swing-arm the new Softail had the look of a Hardtail without the harsh ride. The first true factory cruiser was just around the corner, created by mating the new pseudo-Hardtail frame with more of the California Classic styling cues seen earlier.

56 Harley-Davidson '88 FXDWG
© Harley-Davidson

57 Two choppers by Pat Kennedy,
58 Arizona

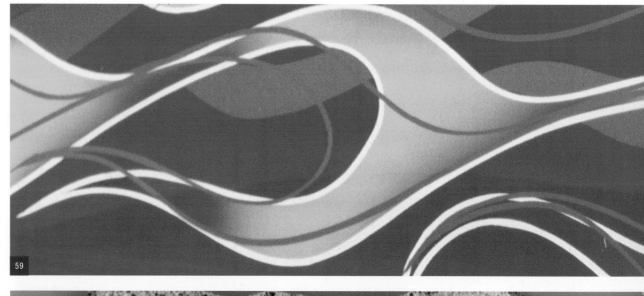

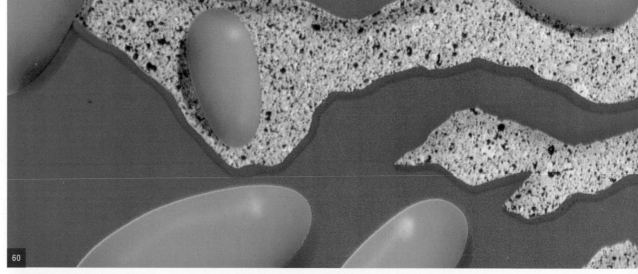

Tank details:

59 *Flamed Chopper*
by Arlen Ness

60 *Flight DeVille*
by Tank Ewsichek

61 *Purple Roadster*
by Dave Perewitz

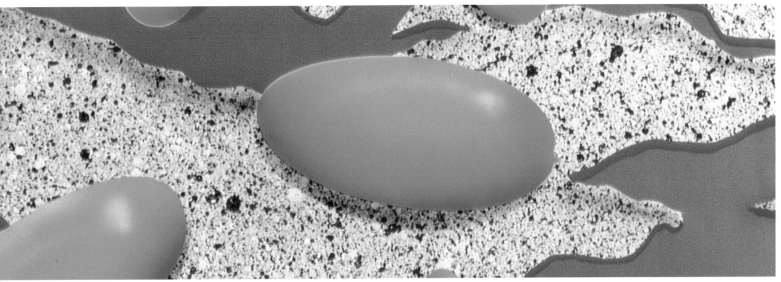

Most industry insiders agree that the creation of the Softail and all the models based on that frame was the best marketing move ever made by Harley-Davidson. The Softail chassis served as the foundation for at least four families of successful bikes. Before that time they had the sound that everyone wanted, afterwards they had the sound *and* the look that defines an American motorcycle.

The mid and late 1980s weren't a good time for the aftermarket industry. The new customs coming from Milwaukee at the time weren't really custom, but they were radical enough for most riders. Customising your bike meant adding a few chrome accessories or possibly repainting the sheet metal. Custom builders like Dave Perewitz kept their operations small and built bikes for a select group of clients.

It wasn't until about 1990 that the tide really turned and riders were once again working hard to make an individual state-ment with their motorcycles. Each year since 1990 has been better than the one before. More new bikes sold, more people looking to improve their bikes, and more offerings from the aftermarket.

And now it's back, the same only differ-ent. Though the kids have got older, each one still needs a Harley, and each of these machines needs to be different from all the rest. The lust for Harley-Davidsons is so bad that people wait in line for two or three years to get one. Once they own the bike, changes take place quickly. Off comes the sheet metal, on go new parts and fresh wild paint schemes.

Milwaukee can barely keep up with the demand for bikes, much less the demand for individualised bikes with billet forward controls, teardrop air cleaners and stretched Fatbob tanks. Thus the small custom shops and customisers who started out in the 1970s or earlier are looking for larger facilities and more mechanics and painters.

All the large American aftermarket companies have now established a working relationship with at least one well-known

62 *Dyna Glide* by Dave Perewitz, built for Drag Specialties

62

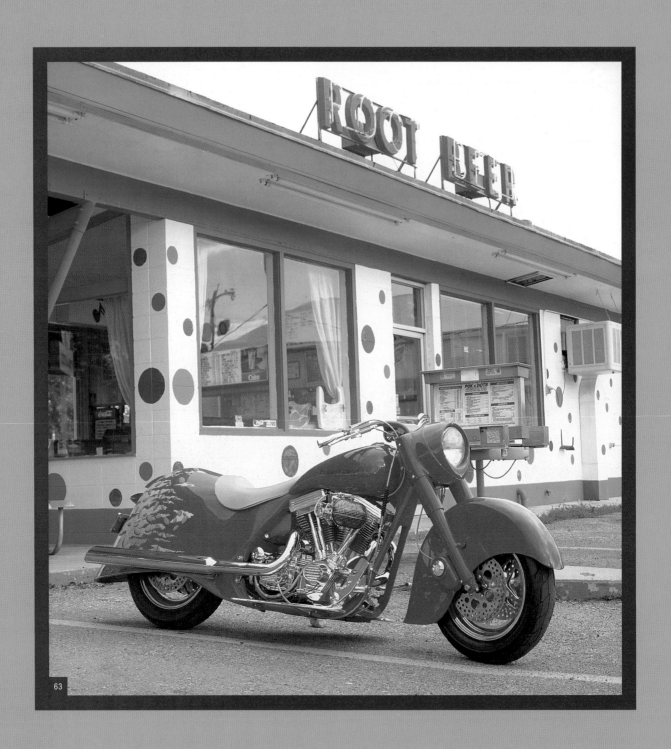

63

63 *Flight DeVille*
by Tank Ewsichek

64 The two *HogZZilla* bikes
by Bauder & Chapouris

65 *HogZZilla*
by Bauder & Chapouris

67 *Eclipse* by Rick Doss,
built for Custom Chrome

68 Rick Doss

66

custom bike builder. Custom Chrome, the biggest of the aftermarket suppliers, rely on well-known customiser Rick Doss for new exhaust pipe and dashboard designs. Drag Specialties use Don Hotop to provide them with fresh new ideas for taillights and hardware. In addition to their work with the best-known builders, each of these companies buys designs on a case-by-case basis from freelance fabricators and designers. Nearly all the companies maintain good relations with the king of American customising, Arlen Ness, who, with help from son Cory, puts out hundreds of new trend-setting parts each year.

A nice feature of these relationships is the fact that most Rick Doss or Don Hotop designs are sold under their own label. Thus the new exhaust pipes in the catalogue are listed as a 'Rick Doss' custom part or 'Don Hotop' design.

This corporate recognition seems an affirmation of the important role these individuals play in a very healthy industry. Without them there might not be four or five major companies selling everything from TailDragger fenders to billet aluminium running boards. They set the styles, create something for all the riders to shoot for – and provide proof that it can be done.

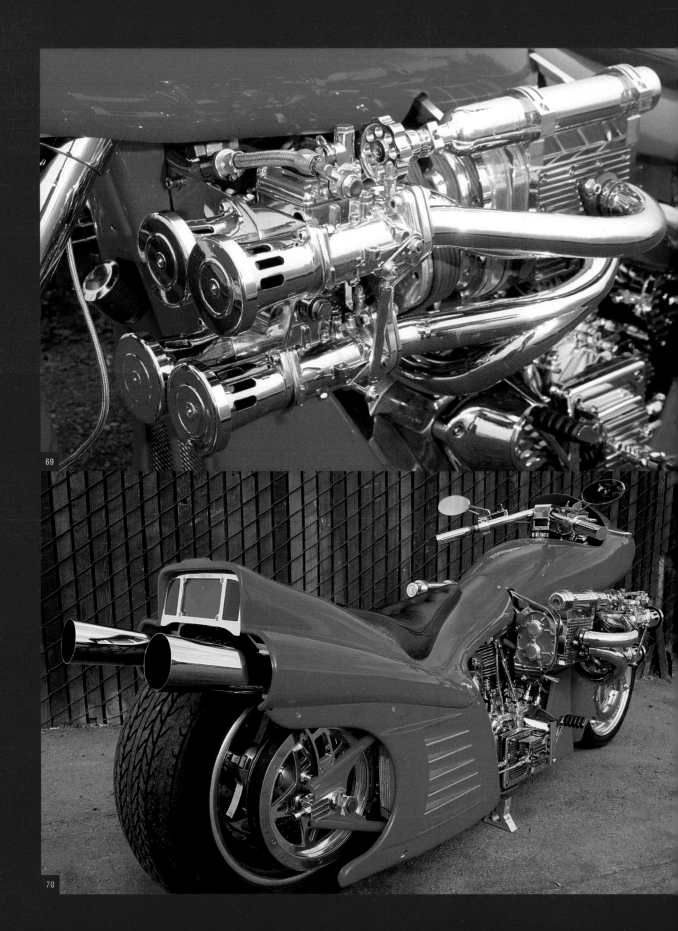

69

70

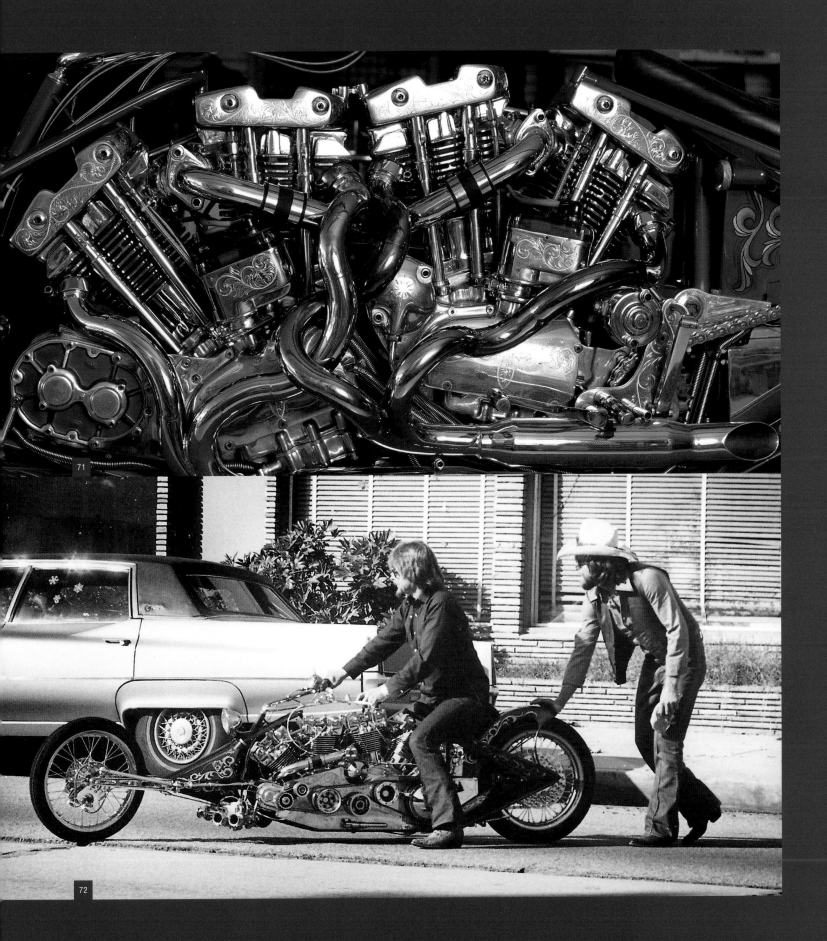

74

Recent converts to the fold, riders astride their first Sportster or Softail think this whole phenomenon is new – that Rick Doss or Arlen Ness just started designing bikes, that people just now began raking the frame to push the front wheel out ahead of the bike.

Old-timers know better. The best-known designers and the busiest shops all have roots that date back to the 1960s and earlier. In fact, this whole wave of success being enjoyed by both Harley-Davidson and the aftermarket can be traced back to those exciting days of yesteryear.

Without a group of mechanics and painters building the trick machines of their day, and a certain movie that gave everything a big push, there might not be the custom craze there is today. Everyone involved, from new bike dealers to small customising shops, owes a collective debt to all those men and women from the '60s and '70s who had the guts to stitch up a new seat, bend up an unusual set of bars or rake the neck. They didn't know it at the time, but they laid the foundation for an industry and a phenomenon the likes of which none of them could have imagined at the time.

AN AMERICAN INTERNATIONAL PICTURE
"HELL'S ANGELS '69" X
starring
TOM   JEREMY   CONNY   STEVE
STERN   SLATE   VAN DYKE   SANDOR
76
EASTMAN COLOUR
From ANGLO AMALGAMATED for WARNER-PATHE release

76 Publicity still from
the film *Hell's Angels '69*
with Sonny Barger (far right)

Bal Croce

Harleys over Hollywood

The Golden Age of the Biker Movie

The roots of the biker myth and its celluloid cousin reach back to the First World War. The American airmen who came to duel across the skies of Europe, fed on a diet of comics and radio serials, gave their units garish, glamorous names culled from their common cultural heritage. Names befitting their squadrons, who would tear out of dark skies spitting lead and belching flames from the nozzles of their red-hot guns – names like 'Hell's Angels'.

Fast forward to 1927: Hollywood was churning out silent movies by the hundred, laying a glittering, fairytale trail of celluloid across the country. It was there and then that tool company millionaire Howard Hughes decided he wanted to make movies too. He was a keen pilot and the story he wanted to tell was that of the WW1 'fly-boys', so he put his big bucks to work. Hughes bought eighty-seven planes and hired the best Hollywood talent his money could afford, including the starlet Greta Nissen to play the smouldering lead.

But that same year, the movie business was revolutionised with the arrival of sound. Warner Bros' first 'talkie' production *The Jazz Singer* caused a sensation, so Hughes scrapped all the footage he'd shot and started again. Nissen's heavy Norwegian accent clearly wasn't going to cut it – so Hughes replaced her with the then unknown Jean Harlow, launching a new star and cashing in with a massive box office hit, when the film, titled *Hell's Angels*, was finally released in 1930.

By World War Two, the next generation of aviators who took to the air to do battle – children of the Great Depression – were still reading comics, but now they were movie fans, too. So when the time came to name their squadrons, the title Hughes 'borrowed' from the Forces was taken back, dusted off and once again painted with pride on the sides of their planes. Several squadrons of 'Hell's Angels' flew tours of duty.

After years of fighting, drinking and travelling in an all-male environment, the peace that was reached didn't sit easy with some of the young aviators when they returned from war. On the West Coast, with its warm dry climate and the profusion of army surplus bikes, groups of these tough young airmen and soldiers, who suddenly found themselves with no war to fight, formed clubs and gangs. These gangs started causing trouble up and down the West Coast, and in 1947 at a bike rally held in Hollister, California, some ran riot and besieged the town. Film producer Stanley Kramer read a fictionalised account of the riot and decided it would make a good film, so he bought the rights and commissioned a screenplay. He thought it would be an ideal vehicle for new movie star and method-acting screen sensation Marlon Brando.

Brando and Kramer hung out with some of the gangs, trying to get a handle on the way they thought, how they talked and what motivated them. 'What are you rebelling against, Johnny?' asked Kramer. 'What you got?' came the laconic quip. It went straight into the script.

The film tells the tale of Brando's gang, 'The Black Rebels Motorcycle Club', riding into a small American town, looking for kicks. They find the place too dull, but just as they are about to split, a rival gang – 'The Beetles' – descends on the town, led by Lee Marvin. A fight breaks out and the town is terrorised. The locals try to stop them but their weak, alcoholic sheriff can't cope. The men of the town form a vigilante mob, beat up Brando and accidentally kill another townsman, whose death they try to blame on Brando. When the state police arrive they sort out the trouble and let all the bikers go with a warning.

Originally to be titled *Hot Blood*, the film was released in 1953 as *The Wild One* and immediately determined the stereotypical biker-hoodlum image that would last throughout the decade. It was automatically condemned by outraged, upstanding citizens – so much so that a special postscript scene was tacked on for some areas, in which a statement assured viewers that the bikers

cinema's cycle odyssey. In 1961, Hammer films, best known for its stylish horror films, produced *These Are The Damned*, set in a strange, futuristic British South Coast and starring a youthful Oliver Reed as the leader of a gang of ruthless bikers.

But the best British biker movie was Sidney Furie's *The Leather Boys* (1963). Fresh from his success with the Cliff Richard vehicle *The Young Ones*, Furie adapted Elliot George's gritty book of the same name into a surprisingly bleak and almost documentary-style drama. It focuses on the dead-end lives of North London couple Reggie and Dot (Colin Campbell and Rita Tushingham), who live in a dreary, no-hope environment of urban decay. They marry young and immediately have problems; Reggie's only escape is his bike and the camaraderie of his fellow rockers, and he becomes friendly with Pete (Dudley Sutton) who is always good for a laugh. Pete is gay, and Reggie falls for him – which, despite the censorship restrictions of the day, is put across with subtle clarity. The film ends as bleakly as it started, with the two boys running away to sea together, but when Reggie meets two old queens in a pub and realises what lies ahead, he leaves, all alone in the world.

In America, in the same year, maverick avant-garde film-maker Kenneth Anger (whose films included the surreal, homoerotic *Fireworks*) filmed his most accessible movie so far, *Scorpio Rising*, a ground-breaking art-house movie that combined the fetishistic rituals of biker culture – pulling on the 'uniform' of jeans, boots and leather jacket, polishing the gleaming bikes – all to an ironic soundtrack of current pop songs (the first time pop music was used purely as a movie soundtrack). Anger crystallised the biker/rebel image by intercutting his shots of bikers drag-racing on a bridge with old footage of dirt track racing, Brando and Dean (taken from TV!), and even some footage from an old black-and-white Sunday school film. In typical Anger fashion, Jesus rides into Nazareth on a donkey – to the tune of The Crystals' 'He's a Rebel'.

were later brought to justice – and it was banned in this country until the 1960s.

It is Lee Marvin, astride a 1950s *Hydra Glide*, with his boozed-up gang of degenerates who were to become more identifiable as 'bikers' as they came to be known in the '60s, dressed in bizarre hats and crazy sunglasses. In fact, the president of the San Francisco Angels drove to Hollywood and somehow managed to get his hands on the blue and yellow striped jumper that Marvin wore in the movie. He wore it until it fell to pieces.

American International Pictures (AIP) dealt with the subject in a couple of the low budget black-and-white flicks they churned out, *Motorcycle Gang* (1957) and *Dragstrip Riot* (1958), but these were pretty tame, teenage offerings. Meanwhile, other areas of the media picked up on the craze. Bikers roared onto the TV screens of America in an episode of *The Twilight Zone* entitled 'Black Leather Jackets', but the three Harley-riding leather-clad dudes were (of course) from outer space. In the pop charts we had The Cheers' 'Black Denim Trousers and Motorcycle Boots' in 1955 and later The Shangrilas' 'Leader of the Pack'.

Surprisingly, it was a couple of British films in the early '60s that continued

Marlon Brando in *The Wild One*. This publicity still has become an icon for a generation of motor-cycle riders

Publicity still from the British bike movie *The Leather Boys*

But on Hollywood's doorstep, things were happening that would make the studios sit up and take notice. The various motorcycle gangs who had been the blueprint for *The Wild One* had continued to flourish, but since the late '40s, a tough, uncompromising biker elite had emerged and once again the name Hells Angels was in the news.

The first chapters were set up in San Bernardino in 1948, San Francisco in '54 and Oakland in '57. By the mid-'60s, some of the more lurid scandal sheets began running shock horror stories on their depraved doings. Hunter S. Thompson made a name for himself by riding with them, writing about them, and eventually falling out with them, penning *Hell's Angels – The Strange and Terrible Saga of Outlaw Motorcycle Gangs* (1966).

Things started warming up in 1965 when Russ Meyer, who had turned his penchant for large-breasted women into big box-office bucks by making tame nudist films, was on the lookout for a new kind of box-office sensation. He thought the bikers would make a good story and filmed *Motor Psycho*, the tale of three crazed bikers on a rape and murder spree. Unfortunately, budgetary restrictions meant they were issued with three pathetic 50cc scooters and their menacing presence was somewhat tarnished.

Back at AIP though, legendary director Roger Corman espied an article on an Angels funeral in *Life* magazine, and the image of this hairy horde of Angels astride their gleaming hogs seemed ripe for exploitation.

Corman had come up through the ranks, starting with ultra-cheap westerns and war dramas and absurd sci-fi and horror films in the late '50s. His proven box-office track record enabled him to get AIP to spring for bigger budgets, and in the early '60s he started a cycle of lush, colourful films based on the works of Edgar Allan Poe. He gathered around him a team of young hopeful talent including Jack Nicholson, Peter Fonda and Peter Bogdanavitch.

In 1966, work started on *All the Fallen Angels* (later retitled *The Wild Angels*). Like the writers of *The Wild One* before them, they

went and met groups of the Angels and enlisted their support, although the relationship was always an uneasy one (Bogdanavitch was reputedly stomped by a gang during filming). The film was shot in a documentary style, following the ruthless, crazed antics of Peter Fonda and his gang as they drink, fight, get high and scream around on their chopped hogs. Their film offers no counterpoint to their mindless violence, no contrived Hollywood sermonising – the gang were just seen to rage out of control and get away with it.

Fonda was a last-minute choice as gang leader – the role was set aside for George Chakaris, but Corman wanted realism and insisted Chakaris ride a Harley. He couldn't comply and so was replaced by Fonda (astride a resplendent Panhead, with springer front end and Fatbob tank). He was joined by a rather wooden-looking Nancy Sinatra, and Bruce Dern, in a show-stealing performance, is their scuzzball buddy 'Loser', whose death gave Corman a chance to recreate the funeral that inspired the movie. In church, a priest starts preaching at the Angels about the evils of their ways, so they stomp him, hold an orgy in the church and then bury their pal – having gang-raped his girlfriend. The gang flees a group of outraged locals before the police arrive but Fonda

81 Album cover for
The Wild Angels soundtrack

stays behind to take the rap because 'there's nowhere to go'.

The critics howled with indignation at this crass exploitation trash but audiences went crazy for it. Davey Allen and The Arrows' bongo-driven theme tune was a smash hit, and AIP made the biggest profits that it had ever seen. The Angels were not best pleased with the film's portrayal of them as mindless thugs and (unsuccessfully) sued AIP for four million dollars in damages for showing them in a 'false and derogatory manner'.

Every exploitation film-maker in the land dropped what they were doing and rushed copycat films into production to milk the latest Hollywood cash cow – or should that be hog? AIP themselves followed it up with *Devil's Angels* (1967), a carbon copy of its predecessor, in which John Cassavetes played Cody, an older, more world-weary gang leader. Although scripted by *Wild Angels* writer Charles Griffith, the violence is toned down, and despite some gang rampages, the tone of the film is less anarchic and mindless and ends with Cody driving into the sunset with a tear in his eye. Hollywood wannabes Dennis Hopper and Bruce Dern join the fun, making this another ground-breaking moment in the biker genre.

More of interest to biker fans was Joe Solomon's effort of that year, *Hell's Angels On Wheels*. He did a deal with Hells Angels president Sonny Barger, who appeared in a cameo role and acted as 'consultant'. Solomon employed cinematographer Laszlo Kovacs, and in an opening scene, a stunningly shot cavalcade of hundreds of real-life Angels roars off on a run across the Golden Gate Bridge. Adam Roarke plays Buddy, the leader of a chapter of the Angels, and his group hook up with Poet (Jack Nicholson), who falls for Buddy's girlfriend. She alternately encourages him (every time Buddy makes out with a go-go dancer) and leaves him (when Buddy wants her back). Poet doesn't understand her but hangs around for assorted fights, orgies and murders, until he and Buddy duel it out in a

THE GLORY STOMPERS

X

DENNIS HOPPER JODY McCREA CHRIS NOEL JOCK MAHONEY

Eton Films presents an American International Picture

3" S/C   Hire Fee 75p

climactic fight in which Buddy dies. Poet retires confused.

Other biker films churned out in the golden year of 1967 include *The Rebel Rousers*, also with Nicholson, Bruce Dern and Diane Ladd (both from *The Wild Angels*), Harry Dean Stanton and Cameron Mitchell. A dream cast, shot by Laszlo Kovacs, but nonetheless a turkey. Also released were *The Wild Rebels* and another AIP effort, *Born Losers*. Kovacs was again employed by schlock-master Al Adamson to film *Hell's Bloody Devils*, a mess only notable for a rare on-screen appearance by Kentucky Fried Chicken's Col. Saunders.

The throttle was kept full open in 1968, when Dennis Hopper returned as leader of 'The Black Souls' in *The Glory Stompers*, joined

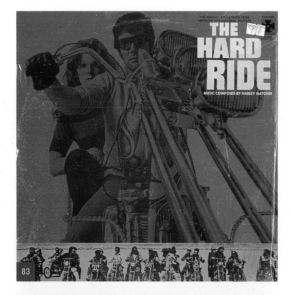

by Bing Crosby's son Lindsay, wise-talking DJ Casey Kasem and another of *The Wild Angels'* Davey Allan's soundtracks.

AIP also rushed out one of the earliest 'girls on bikes' flicks, *The Mini Skirt Mob*, about an all-girl gang of Honda-riding side-kicks to some bike-riding rodeo cowboys. They terrorise an old friend for marrying out of the gang (aided by, amongst others, Harry Dean Stanton again). Dick Clark (*The American Bandstand* supremo) produced *The Savage Seven* for AIP, featuring Adam Roarke and a cameo by guitar legend Duane Eddy. After huge box-office success with *Hell's Angels On Wheels*, AIP also asked Joe Solomon to be executive producer on another biker movie for them that year, *Angels From Hell*. Jack Starrett played a cop out to get a gang led by a Vietnam veteran (Tom Stern). By now the formula was wearing a little thin and once again we get fights, orgies, run-ins with the law and a final showdown.

Veteran exploitation film-maker Herschell Gordon Lewis – who, together with David Friedman, had invented the 'gore' movie with *Blood Feast* – wanted to duplicate the box-office success of these movies and thought a shit-kicking gang of all-girl-Harley-riding-babes – mixed with 'gouts of blood' – would fit the bill. He was right, and *She Devils On Wheels* became his biggest hit in years. Lewis didn't bother with actors – he just advertised for girls who could ride big bikes, and he scripted a number of scenarios where they beat up guys, had sex with willing studs and recited limericks to cops. The result was a biker classic that is still doing business on video nearly thirty years later.

In Europe, cinematographer Jack Cardiff took the director's seat and tried to sum up the spirit of the late '60s in a movie that could have almost beaten *Easy Rider* to the draw as biker/art movie of the decade – had it not been so downright weird and quite frankly dull. The Anglo-French *Girl On A Motorcycle* sees Marianne Faithfull driving around a psychedelic Europe on a huge black Harley in a one-piece leather catsuit (hence

its American title *Naked Under Leather*). At the end of the film she gets so excited by the vibration of the throbbing bike between her legs that she loses control and dies, just as this movie did at the box office.

By the end of the '60s, America was in big trouble, with the Vietnam war at its height and the civil rights campaign tearing the country apart. Many of the more innovative film makers such as Corman had moved on, leaving a mainly second-rate bunch of sleaze merchants to churn out more and more derivative and uninspired biker fare.

1969 saw another AIP attempt at an all-girl biker movie, *Hell's Belles*, and Pat Barrington (cult star of *Orgy Of The Dead* and *Mondo Topless*) stepped out with a lesbian gang in *Sisters In Leather*. Casey Kasem and Davie Allen were still at it in *Wild Wheels*, and director Bill Brame managed to pull one of the most bizarre cast twists ever in his dope fiend/biker no-hit movie *Free Grass*, by getting Russ Tamblyn, Richard Breymer and Natalie Wood's sister Lana together and ballyhooing the whole mess with adverts screaming 'See the stars of *West Side Story*, together again on the big screen'. Al Adamson (director of *Hell's Bloody Devils*) couldn't believe that such a (once) big Hollywood name as Tamblyn would stoop to being in such trash, and immediately signed him for his new film *Satan's Sadists*, perhaps one of the most vicious, humourless and unsavoury stories of a gang of bikers raping, killing and drinking their way across small-town America. By now, nudity (which was uncommon in the earlier biker movies) was more acceptable, and *Naked Angels* is worthy of a mention as the biker movie with the most flesh flashed across the screen.

As the decade drew to a close, there were three biker flicks of relative merit, worthy of more scrutiny. *Hell's Angels '69* was produced by Tom Stern and directed by Lee Maden, who were also the film's stars, playing a couple of swinging Las Vegas bachelors who come up with an Ocean's 11-inspired plot to rip off a casino. They disguise themselves as bikers and fall in with a bunch of Hells

Angels who they befriend with ludicrous ease. They duly pull off the heist with the aid of the bikers, who they then double-cross. The bikers realise they have been ripped off and track the duo down for a climactic show-down. Whilst well shot and edited, and a story much more palatable than many previously mentioned, the real strength of this film lies in the casting – the Angels are played by Sonny Barger and his buddies. For fans of biker movies who enjoyed the Hunter S. Thompson book, it's great to see all the real-life characters riding, partying and generally having a ball on screen.

Joe Solomon (*Hell's Angels On Wheels* and

Losers (1970), as Smith and biker regular Adam Roarke drive around Cambodia on armoured dirt bikes creating mayhem. Smith was also in the unremarkable *C.C. & Company* the same year.

But the film of 1969 that stands out as not only one of the best biker movies, but certainly one of the most influential and greatest counterculture movies ever, is *Easy Rider*. Hopper, Nicholson and Fonda were in the middle of a creative vortex of Hollywood hipsters – acting, writing and producing a bewildering number of arty and experimental films. Corman dropped acid to direct Fonda and Hopper in the Nicholson-scripted drug flick *The Trip* (1967). Dick Clark produced *Psych-Out* in 1968 starring Nicholson (along with biker regulars Bruce Dern, Adam Roarke and Dean Stockwell) which was directed by Richard Rush (*The Savage Seven* and *Hell's Angels On Wheels*), again with cinematographer Laszlo Kovacs.

When Hopper and Fonda went to the AIP honchos with the script for *Easy Rider*, they refused to let the erratic Hopper direct. Columbia had no such misgivings and stumped up the cash. Less about rampaging Harley-riding Neanderthals and more about free spirits, exploration, freedom and the decay in the belly of America, *Easy Rider* went on to become the biggest-grossing independent movie ever made. It struck a chord with a whole generation and shook up a complacent Hollywood, who once again tried to jump on the bandwagon.

Besides the well-crafted and sensitively handled script and Nicholson's barnstorming portrayal of a drunken lawyer, Laszlo Kovacs' cinematography almost steals the show. Hopper's fully customised bike weaving through bursts of sun flare, and Fonda on his gleaming Harley V-twin Panhead, with stars and stripes painted on his tank, blasting through the great mid-West, raked forks to the fore – on the sort of trip every rebel would like to take.

Easy Rider really was the zenith of the biker movie, the end of a trip that had taken us from Brando's leather jacketed rebel,

Angels From Hell) still believed in biker box office, and he let Jack Starrett make the move from playing a cop, up into the director's chair, casting the legendary William Smith in the lead for *Run Angel Run*. The impressively muscled – and untypically bright – Smith makes this well-crafted movie believable, playing a disgruntled biker who sells his gang's story to a tabloid so he can afford to start a new life. His old gang go after him for spilling the beans and, with some impressive stunts and story twists along the way, they catch him up for a chain-whipping showdown. Solomon and Starrett had Smith back in the saddle the next year for their fourth biker movie, *The Losers*. Sonny Barger had genuinely written to President Johnson in 1965, offering the services of 'a crack group of' Angels to go to Vietnam to help the war effort. The President chose not to take up the offer, but Solomon and Starrett filmed what might have been in

through an orgy of cycle destruction and mayhem, to a cool and hip conclusion of Hopper and Fonda's characters, whose American dream is blasted off the road by bigoted shotgun-toting rednecks. The release of the film documentary *Gimme Shelter* (1970) sounded the death knell for any future attempts to glorify the doings of Hells Angels, when the audience at the Rolling Stones' free festival at Altamont witnessed the grim, depressing conclusion to their 'Summer Of Love' dream, as the Angels (who were hired as security for the event) bashed heads, stomped hippies with pool cues and eventually stabbed to death an eighteen-year-old kid who had threatened Jagger with a gun.

More ludicrous biker movies were nonetheless churned out: in 1970 a young Jonathan Demme cut his teeth as director of *Angels Hard As They Come*; a gang of (real-life) black bikers slug it out with white rivals in the ultra-violent *Black Angels*; and other nonsense includes *Angels Die Hard*, *Angels Unchained* and *Wild, Free and Hungry*.

By 1971 things were drying up. The promising idea of mixing a horror theme with bikers was explored in the magnificently titled (but inept in every other way) *Werewolves On Wheels*. A British film of the next year tried to fit in this market with more success. *Psychomania* tells the story of a young David Hemmings who discovers the secret of immortality. He imparts this knowledge to his gang and they all become a zombie biker gang called 'The Living Dead'. By now, most American biker movies were made for the drive-in circuit and featured lots of blood, violence and sex. The British production of *Psychomania* – with the BBFC to contend with – seemed comparatively staid. The gang's shocking high jinks consisted of knocking bags of shopping out of housewives' hands and sticking their tongues out at policemen. However, it remains an interesting and entertaining film with some good stunts.

The biker movie was really dead by the early '70s (no biker films were produced in 1975 or 1976), but a few notable exceptions

either paid homage to the genre or tried to revive it. Besides tired and uninspired movies like 1973's *Bury Me Angel*, which featured a pre-Grizzly Adams Dan Haggerty, and *Hex*, where John and Keith Carradine try to sprinkle their family magic on the biker genre with no result, a few succeeded. The same year, the dreams of a short-ass motorcycle cop were explored in the arty *Electra Glide In Blue*. 1977 saw the release of *The Northville Cemetery Massacre*. A classic biker movie of the old school, filmed in Detroit, with the cops as the villains and bikers the good guys, a cast of unknown, but talented, actors play out the superbly told story to background music scored by The Monkees' Mike Nesbit! Eight years later, the Angels themselves released a movie – having taken ten years to complete it – by themselves, about themselves. Called *Hells Angels Forever*, this excellent documentary is a must for biker fans and features appearances from Bo Didley and Willie Nelson.

Besides such abominations as *I Bought A Vampire Motorbike* and *Harley-Davidson And The Marlborough Man*, other vaguely bike-themed films appeared occasionally, such as a gay biker movie, *Pink Angels*, and of course porn, for example *Sleazy Rider*.

But one of the last truly classy biker flicks was Kathryn Bigelow's *The Loveless* (1981). Set in the '50s, it gives a retro-cool, nostalgic look at what it was about *The Wild One* that made it so terminally hip to be a biker. Featuring wannabe rockabilly crooner Robert Gordon and an early appearance from Willem Dafoe, *The Loveless* conjures up a golden age of suspender belts, leather jackets and gleaming vintage Harleys, with pop promo sensibilities, and it seems to take us full circle to the roots of the biker myth.

The biker movie cycle, which started in 1953 with *The Wild One*, has seemingly run out of gas, but in its brief blaze across the silver screen, biker movies led the way, from the leather-clad Johnny, mumbling defiance at the small-town squares, to *The Wild Angels*, although now almost forgotten by all but the most ardent fans of the genre, one of the most shocking and seminal movies of its day (it was chosen as the American entry to Cannes). They gave breaks to stars who are now legends, such as Hopper, Nicholson, Fonda (as well as a host of others – Harry Dean Stanton, Oliver Reed, John Cassavetes, Diane Ladd, Adam Roarke and Dean Stockwell) and of course Brando.

Easy Rider still has the cinematic vision to inspire all who watch it, an irresistible cocktail of freedom, cool and rebellion, and the imagery of the bikes flying across the vast American plains is what it is all about. Recently clear of a long-running legal battle, it is now free to air on TV, and is available on video. If you want to capture what the essence of biker culture is about, get it, or indeed many of the other films recommended above.

91 Dennis Hopper and Peter Fonda riding custom choppers in the film *Easy Rider*

92 *Easy Rider* film poster

93 Still from *Easy Rider*. Fonda rushes to help Hopper, who is shot in the final scene of the movie

Sources: *The Psychotronic Encyclopaedia Of Film* (Michael Weldon), *The Psychotronic Video Guide* (Michael Weldon), *Cycle Cinema* (Greg Hinderycs) – article: 'Filmfax #27, Attack Of The Cycle Psychos' (Steve Puchalski) and article: 'Shock X-Press' Vol. 2, Issue 5.

Ian Mutch

European
Custom
Harleys

The custom scene that hit Europe in the wake of the mind-altering movie *Easy Rider* was as fundamental to the appearance and attitude of motorcycling as the Reformation was to the established church.

British motorcycles, pre-Peter Fonda, were characterised by short low bars and big fuel tanks crowned with chins, above which gritted teeth underlined goggled eyes glued to the speedo in lustful anticipation of witnessing the magic ton.

The post-*Easy Rider* world, by contrast, totally reassessed the motorcycle, not as a means of achieving high speed, but of indulging self-expression both in the motorcycle itself and in a reinterpreted life of unfettered travel and freedom. The influence of the '60s with its anarchical mould-breaking essence was reflected by the mechanical form of the motorcycle in a manner that provoked outrage and contempt among the established legions of silk-scarved rockers and classic buffs alike. We didn't get it right at once. The infancy of the European custom art spawned a legion of motorised abortions inspired by vague visual concepts allied to a minimum of engineering know-how.

Several criteria culled from the American chopper image survived the transatlantic crossing to be grafted onto the still Brit-based UK bike scene, resulting in humorous amalgams of mostly amateur endeavour. What the *Easy Rider* wannabes could identify were, first and foremost, long forks and high bars. Splice those two elements into a project, and, in the eyes of the disciples, you had a chopper.

The other essential factor was low seats – low was cool, and yet, ironically, in pursuit of that, the hasty pioneers frequently sacrificed their goal through failing to understand that only by raking the frame could such ground-hugging qualities be reconciled with the desired long forks. Without raking the frame, that is to say altering the angle of the headstock to which the forks are attached, the longer forks simply lifted the whole front end of the bike, disturbing its

96

97

geometry and ruining the handling while raising bums even higher off the tarmac than they had been before.

In an effort to counter this effect, the custom market offered sparsely padded banana seats to replace the fatter standard items. Typically, these were married to unsympathetic frames using desperate contrivances of bolts, with hacksaws and dexion playing roles in mechanical follies that concluded with the seats peeling upwards like sun-dried leaves, only to be re-secured with lashings of wire.

More ambitious builders welded rigid or Hardtail frame sections in lieu of the standard sub-frames with their swinging arm suspension systems, in an effort to lower their bikes. The less thorough simply substituted solid struts for their suspension units, lowering the back of the bike close to the tyre

without allowing it to foul the mudguard. Proper motorcyclists poured derision on the fad, but the new wave riders didn't care. Their hands were high and their front wheels rode ahead of them like monarchs' heralds; it was a case of never mind the quality, cop the length. Happy days.

Survival of this embryonic culture, in the face of critical broadsides from performance buffs and safety critics, owes much to the liberal interpretation of MOT stations and the sluggish response from legislators in those early days. As custom pioneer John Reed (Uncle Bunt) once said, 'We were damn lucky to get through that period without major interference from parliament.' Not all experiments of that era were so unprofessional, however, and it would be remiss to ignore the efforts of conspicuous British instigators like the builder–painter Ray Leon and frame-builder John Wallace, noteworthy prophets of the art who sculpted credible creations which stood head and shoulders above the herd. Also conspicuous among the early runners was Dave Batchelar of P&D, frame-makers of distinction who are still operating today, as is Jake's Motique, a Harley-Davidson custom emporium in Surrey. More recent players include the likes of restorer and custom builder Richard Taylor, Jeff Murphy of Riverside Cycles, East Coast Cycles, Phil Piper and Gus Traegus. In the final finish department, paintwork maestros like Ty Lawer of Pageant Paint, Matt the Painter and Ken Rothery have brought their exceptional talents to top coat many of this country's finest.

Inevitably, the gregarious nature of bikers spawned a major custom club in the shape of the National Chopper Club (NCC) founded in the early '70s. A tight-knit group, though not a back patch (outlaw)

98 Norton rider at a Rockers' reunion, Chelsea Bridge, 1984

99 Members of the National Chopper Club, BMF rally, 1991

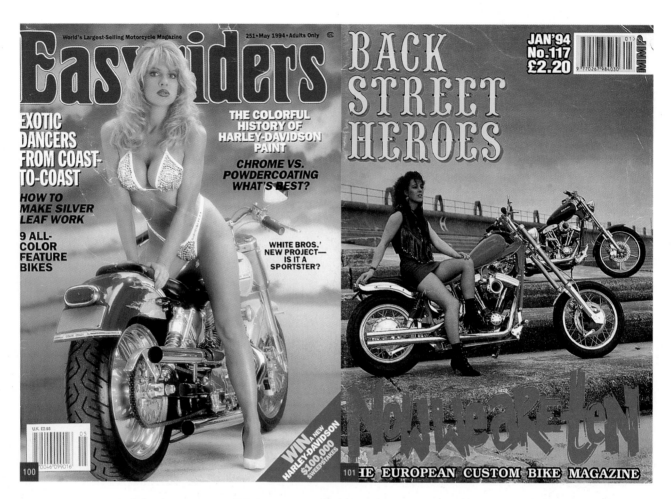

club, they were established as a partyin' and riding club, with ownership of a custom motorcycle a central condition of membership. As a single innovative group, they have probably contributed more to the custom scene than any other over the years.

In 1979 the Hells Angels (a back patch club) organised Britain's first bikes-only custom motorcycle show, the Kent Custom Bike Show, which was an instant success and grew rapidly year on year, attracting attendances of over 20,000 for a weekend of partyin', the focal point of which was the custom show itself, which attracted entrants from across Europe. Many more shows hosted by a variety of organisers were to follow.

By the '80s, the custom bike-building art had established itself as a credible faction within the motorcycle sphere. Since the early '70s, the imaginations of builders had been fuelled by the American magazine *Easyriders*. A hard title to get hold of, it was full of wild bikes and outrageous lifestyle pictures. By

1983, Britain's first uncompromising custom/lifestyle magazine, *Back Street Heroes*, hit the newsstands with immediate success. It not only reflected the custom market but catalysed it into overdrive, lending a cohesive impetus to the British custom scene through recognising the aspirations of its readers and applauding the talents of the new wave of bespoke gurus. Billed as 'the European custom bike magazine', it soon faced competition from others like *Big Twin* in Holland, *Freeway* in France, and the German title *High Performance*, while back home and into the late '80s, *HOG* magazine (later renamed *Vee* to avoid copyright infringement with Harley-Davidson) appeared, only to be superseded by *Heavy Duty*, a Harley magazine which has enjoyed several owners throughout its chequered history.

The first custom bikes were British; Triumphs and BSAs for the most part in the earliest days, with Japanese bikes creeping in later in the '70s as their acceptance as

100 *Easyriders* magazine

101 *Back Street Heroes* magazine

102 *Twin Blower* by Richard Taylor

103 *Silver Trike* by Danny Franssen (overleaf)

serious contenders became widespread. Anyone who had a Harley-Davidson in those days was revered as a person of almost mystical quality from another culture. Few would have believed then, that little more than ten years on, the great American freedom machine would sweep Europe with a force not seen since the D-Day landings.

For many years Harley-Davidson had, notwithstanding the Sportster models, led their range with heavyweight machines featuring massive fenders, screens, pannier boxes and saddles, that subordinated the engine, despite its size, to a status of comparative inconsequence. It took Harley-Davidson years to capitalise on the fact that owners were stripping or 'chopping' all this extraneous fibreglass off, to leave a pruned animal with a wheel at each end. Their first attempt at emulating the owner's interpretations of their product was the Super Glide, which was basically just an engine with a wheel at each end. British

bikers, with their nimble snarling parallel twins, had scorned the 'overweight but not many over here yet' behemoths, but with the advent of the Super Glide, a limited number of new wave bikers were tempted onto American iron.

By the dawn of the '90s, and against the spiteful wishes of detractors, the Harley invasion had overwhelmed the European custom scene. The real beachhead was established in the mid-'80s when the new Evolution-engined models caught on big time, attracting a new breed of better-heeled converts and born-again bikers. At long last Harley-Davidson were building bikes that could make fuss-free journeys without the accompaniment of oil tankers and frequent recourse to the tool kit. There was even a range of rubber-mounted options that largely isolated the rider from the V-twin engine's celebrated vibrations for which journalists had articulated so many euphemisms.

Magazines and shows introduced Britain to the long-forked Swedish chops with their uncompromising rigid frames, huge square section back tyres and minimalist design

104 Harley Owners Group
club patch

105 *Yellow Hammer*
by Steve Morley

RUNS ON YUPPIES

HH
EU 1

106   107

106 A HOG family at a Harley
Owners Group rally,
Goodwood, 1993

107 A German custom Harley at
Kent Custom Bike Show, 1997

criteria. Swedish engineering impressed and influenced many builders who recognised their symmetry, line and quality. For years, the Harley scene in Europe was dominated by the Northern countries, with Sweden conspicuous by its extraordinarily high ratio of devotees to population, while Holland boasted many aficionados and a high number of old military models that were mostly chopped. As time passed, Germany became a major force on the scene which spread rapidly south through Europe as the Harley bug bit deeper, fostered by attractive marketing, of which the HOG (Harley Owners Group) was a critical feature. There had been a rider-led club, The Harley-Davidson Riders Club, in many European countries for decades, and though emphatically not an outlaw club, it possesses a raunchiness to which the company wished to provide an alternative. HOG was something different. Founded and funded partly by the Motor Company, HOG established a clean, non-sexist family image, with good rally facilities but no wet T-shirt contests.

In the past, with the exception of a small band of dyed-in-the-wool enthusiasts, Harleys had been associated with the outlaw element. The uniquely brutish appeal of Harleys proved attractive to the overtly macho members of back patch clubs who patronised the marque and resented the invasion of their culture by the yuppies and RUBs (rich urban bikers), who soon outnumbered the great unwashed from whom the Harley-Davidson company were endeavouring to distance themselves. Once, a typical Harley rider would have been a scruffy, oily-fingered and impecunious devotee for whom the motorcycle was the one thing of beauty and value in his life. The new Harley owner is likely to be a company director, solicitor, or graphic artist, who uses his Harley for fun in the sun and his Porsche or Range Rover at other times. While traditional patrons have not been displaced, they have been outnumbered by the better heeled as the status of motorcycling in general and Harley-riding in particular, has grown.

The proliferation of Harley-Davidson

108

109

brothers Ricky and Dean, in conjunction with French ex-pat Jeff Duval and partner Nigel Saxon, founded Battistinis Custom Cycles of Bournemouth. The company rapidly built a series of stunningly stylish Harley customs. Word of the South Coast crucible of creativity spread rapidly as custom magazines turned their lenses on the bewildering succession of long, lean, low customs rolling out of the cobbled yard off Grand Parade.

Within a year, Battistinis had established their signature. Slender stretched frames devoid of ugly lugs, pullback handlebar risers, exquisitely tapered fuel tanks, an abundance of high quality parts and a finish to challenge the magnifying glasses of the most fastidious critics. Bikes of this class don't come cheap, a typical Battistini product commanding prices between £20,000 and £30,000. What also distinguished Battistinis from many custom builders was an ability to deliver to a timetable. Where many artisans would keep customers waiting months or even years as they fitted projects between other jobs and waited eternities for parts shipments, Battistinis could accelerate the process to satisfy clients who had the dosh and wanted the goods *tout de suite*.

The inspiration for the business grew partly from the frustration of lengthy waits for custom parts to be shipped from the USA, where the legendary Arlen Ness led the world with a range of cosmetic interpretations of Harley's components. Faced with such delays but recognising the style and demand for Ness parts, Battistinis invested substantially in stock to meet escalating European demand.

Today, Battistinis' business is almost entirely in parts, with complete bikes built mostly as rolling advertisements for the growing product range of Ness and Battistini items. A testament to the excellence of the company's own creativity lies with the steady order for Battistini fuel tanks by none other than Arlen Ness himself; a curious case of 'coals to Newcastle' that cements the symbiotic relationship of chrome across the ocean.

rallies across Europe, like the French Freewheels, the Harley Riders Super Rallies, and numerous HOG rallies, started tempting the new and affluent owners to cover longer distances on the practical Evo-engined bikes. This steered the custom art onto a more practical tack with a steady decline in the prevalence of rigid frames that had sustained the practices of countless osteopaths and dentists in the preceding decades.

Against this background, a new name erupted onto the custom scene with the impact of Etna. In 1991, the Battistini

Perhaps the biggest influence on the custom scene from the '80s onward has been the acceptance of the custom market by Harley-Davidson and the company's efforts to accommodate owners' aspirations within its model range. For many, this has effectively discouraged the radical customisation that dictated complete frame-builds or fundamental modification in favour of a bolt-on philosophy. While Battistinis continue to build unique bikes, they have been quick to recognise the more moderate appetite for reconciling personal expression with practicality and legality, an objective which can be achieved by tasteful selection of complementary components. While the radical die-hards deride the bolt-on 'cheats', others point to an analogy with our alphabet, which provides writers with infinite scope for expression by artistic combinations of a finite supply of letters. The custom parts catalogues feature far more than the alphabet's twenty-six components, so it should come as little surprise that many permutations of the custom art can be facilitated by their use.

In Northern Europe, a healthy custom scene had been growing in tandem with the British one – most conspicuously in Sweden, where that nation's outward-looking anglified culture had adopted a vicarious patriotism toward both British and American motorcycle products. As in most Western countries, and at the risk of enraging Brit iron aficionados, the rule was: if you can't afford a Harley, get a Triumph or a BSA. Within the custom motorcycle culture of Sweden, most are mystified by the implicitly self-deprecating patronage of Oriental machines by the British.

The Swedes take their custom bikes seriously, crafting them with a thoughtful care that enables respect for their engineering credibility to survive the shock reaction to their radical visual qualities. What has enabled the radical chop to survive in Sweden, while it has declined elsewhere in Europe, is the wonderful quality of the roads. Suspension is really only necessary because most roads have bumps. The Swedes have not only exceptional roads but an exceptional winter that effectively prohibits motorcycle use for eight months of the year and encourages custom builders to spend long evenings in their sheds crafting or reworking their motorcycles for the next riding season.

If there is a criticism of the Swedish style then it lies with a predictability that might lead a gullible alien to believe that Swedish motorcycles *must* have huge car tyres at the

back, rigid frames, and long forks. To court a charge of heresy one might suggest that the Swedes are stuck in a time warp. Then again, there is something reassuring in a nation so clearly retaining a national characteristic against today's pressures of cultural coalescence.

Critics who have assumed that the fangled choppers must be intrinsically unsafe have been confounded by the findings of Swedish insurance companies however, who actually offer reduced premiums to owners of custom-built motorcycles. The simple fact is that owners of custom bikes have less accidents, most probably because they do not have the same obsession with speed that some other bikers have. The Swedish experience bears out the belief that safety is more about riding within the limitations of a machine than with the intrinsic capabilities of that machine.

The Swedish reputation for quality has been sustained by some exceptional builders and component makers, the name of Tolle being synonymous with high-quality forks that look and operate effectively within their geometric limitations; the Heollund Brothers achieved world-wide fame with their frames which sell in over twenty-five countries, while Eriksson's startling 80- and 120-spoke wheels have been copied around the world.

In Britain, the custom scene evolved along more moderate lines, with the lowrider prevailing in preference to the long forked chopper. Lowriders accommodate modified rear suspension systems in tandem with shortened forks, the moderate compromise between a stock bike and the etiolated Swedish extreme, reflecting the traditional British reserve which favours understatement. Such creations tend to draw applause from all parties, even from the more conservative elements who can recognise what they see as a legitimate interpretation of a classic concept.

With the passage of time, the Southern European countries have begun to catch up with their Northern counterparts as the endemic artistic talents of the cultures have found form in the new medium.

To risk generalisation: The Germans have cultivated a look characterised by heavy engineering and aggressive imagery, epitomised by the likes of Fred Kodlin, whose work has made its mark on both sides of the Atlantic, with a 'Best in Show' for his 'Murder Cycle' at Daytona. The French style, with its emphasis on vivid colours, is championed by the likes of Nicolas Chauvin, whose tribute to Stevie Ray Vaughan took

114 115

'Best Bike' at the '92 Kent Show. Odyssey Kolor's Bertrand Dubert is another leading player alongside builder and accessory manufacturers Technoplus with their range of distinctive component options. In Italy there is an emphasis on performance led by craftsmen from companies like Carbon Dream. In Holland, the Lowtail company have produced a range of custom Harley-Davidson frames to accommodate appetites for low seating positions within a workable design, while in Switzerland, Bikers Paradise have brought the precision of the watch-maker to 'no expense spared' machines bristling with roller bearings to minimise friction and maximise efficiency.

Among the aftermarket accessory companies, Zodiac stands out as a conspicuous European operator, offering a wide range of parts to meet increasingly demanding customers. Back in the early '80s they employed British custom motivator and designer John Reed, who went on to work for

US aftermarket giant CCI, while in Germany, W&W lead the pack with a similar catalogue of bewildering possibilities. Of course the danger in mentioning any names lies with the certainty that a thousand will be omitted, and I apologise to the anonymous in advance.

If a single factor, besides the movie *Easy Rider*, has leant direction to the custom art, it

117 *Tribute to Stevie Ray Vaughan* by Nicolas Chauvin

118

Paul Tropman riding his Battistinis custom Harley on the dragstrip at the Bulldog Bash, 1997

is probably the drag scene. Drag bikes, built for tearing up straight strips from a standing start, have long wheelbases and low centres of gravity for straight line stability. The customs that draw on this inspiration, though usually shortened, reflect the look, with low bars dictating a forward-leaning posture. Any comparison with the cafe racer image of the '50s and '60s, however, is denied by the retention of standard or even forward footpeg positions and low seat heights.

The drag-inspired sturdiness of this style draws many admirers, who find its compact muscularity appealing. Wide stubby forks in front of broad tapering fuel tanks with functional aircraft-style flush filler caps, cutting in to narrow hindquarters, give these bikes a lionesque athleticism that is a mile removed from the lazy spideryness of Fonda's gangling chopper. To undertake long journeys with both hands and feet forward of the body, however, is to court agony, and the

consistency with which owners of these bikes defend their practicality as comfortable rides bears testimony to their self-delusion. By the mid-'90s, very wide straight bars, particularly popular in Holland and Germany, had accentuated this image, suggesting the approach of a reversed wedge.

The survival of the German custom motorcycle scene against the bureaucratic obstacles of the Teutonic TÜV system is a monument to resourcefulness, persistence and guile. Acting on the assumption that all modifications of a factory product must be negative, the German government concocted a maze of rules that make it expensive and difficult to register custom machines. In Britain, where the compulsory helmet law had prompted the formation of a riders' movement in the shape of the Motorcycle Action Group (MAG) in 1973, persistent lobbying has kept the threat of legal controls at bay and fostered a dialogue with the

119 *Flame Job*
     by Phil Piper

120 Futuristic custom Harley
     by Hans Boekhoue, Holland

authorities, who have recognised the absence of conflict between bespoke motorcycles and safety. Had this country adopted the German system then most of the less affluent builders would have found their operations obstructed by the need to submit sacrificial examples of frames, handlebars etc. for destruction testing at astronomical cost. Thankfully, the sustained campaign against the helmet law helped to convince legislators that they were dealing with an increasingly organised and vocal lobby which would not evaporate or accept pointless bureaucracy when it interfered with the reasonable expectations for enjoyment of its supporters.

Perhaps the greatest complement to Harley-Davidson's success has been the attempt by others to build look-a-like models with low-slung frames and big V-twin engines: Yamaha's Drag Star, Suzuki's Intruder, Kawasaki's Classic, and Honda's Shadow – even the conservative BMW company has produced a cruiser. However close these clones get to the all-American ideal, though, they remain imitations, and in consequence enjoy the mirthful contempt of those for whom nothing but the real thing will do.

The custom motorcycle world has come a long way from its conceptual days as the product of DIY merchants' enthusiasm, having largely survived both the censure of conservative critics and the threats of unsympathetic bureaucrats bent on conformity. Against the odds, the art form has earned legitimacy across the board, from Harley-Davidson, whose products inspired it, to the Oriental competitors who have aped it. This exhibition bears witness to the reassuring fact that in a world where automotive design is propelled by objective criteria, there are those for whom the motorcycle is more than transport; it is a credible form of artistic self-expression. Long may it continue.

121 Futuristic concept Harley by
Bunt's Motorcycle Company

122

122 *Serial 1*, one of three Harley-Davidson
      motorcycles built in 1903
      © Harley-Davidson

Dr. Martin Jack Rosenblum

Harley-Davidson Aesthetic:

Factory Custom Fine Art and Rider Custom Folk Art

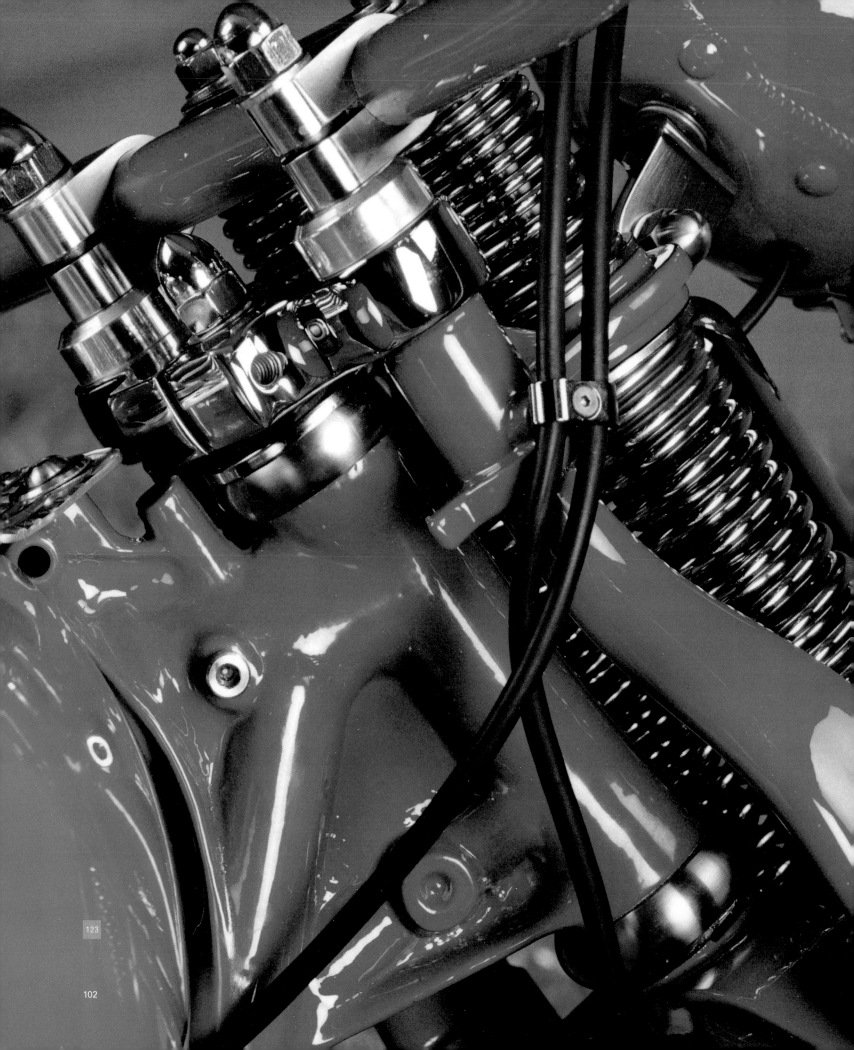

I Authenticity

As with any product that does not merely succeed in the marketplace but also becomes symbolic, creating an iconography that is the item as well as its cultural meanings, the Harley-Davidson motorcycle has achieved technical and philosophical status. While there is, as evinced by the Barbican installation, a considerable and expanding rider custom folk art movement, it is naturally built upon the factory custom fine art

presentation. What is meant by this is that – to quote Willie G. Davidson, Vice President of Styling at the Motor Company – Harley-Davidson motorcycles are 'rolling sculptures'. These magnificent machines, though, have ghosts in them that haunt the rider's imagination. The bikes take possession of the enthusiast such that he or she then brings personal mythology to bear upon how the bike must appear in order to be an expression of individual character.

Harley-Davidsons have souls that encourage their owners to participate in the design process. The individual is inspired to create as a result of what has been obtained from the dealer's showroom floor. The bike travels from showroom to street to the owner's mysterious garage, where folk ritual is performed.

If you have ever entered the sacred territory of the Harley-owner's garage, you have entered an environment that can be tastefully compared to a place of worship. The walls are decorated with various aspects of Harley-Davidson arcana, replete with posters, banners, photographs of rides taken, motorcycle parts (those removed and those to be installed), family memorabilia related to experiences in the Harley universe, tables and shelves of drawings, notes and tools. In the midst of this hallowed ground is the Harley-Davidson motorcycle. Usually, the family four-wheeled vehicle sits in the alley or street or, with the more fortunate homeowners, another corner of the garage.

There is a heater for winter and an air conditioner for summer and, definitely, a refrigerator and coffeemaker. Sometimes there might be a telephone, but communications, while at work on the customisation, are kept to a minimum.

There will be an old military ammo box filled with cleaning and polishing agents, and an orange crate from the 1950s crammed with lubricants. One's wife, husband or children are not allowed to mess around with these elements of ritual. While the Harley-related books and magazines piled on top of the stool in the corner can be carefully paged through, service parts and owners' manuals cannot. The motorcycle itself can never be touched. When it is ridden, let the wind roar and the dirt soar. When the machine is at rest, no fingerprint may be applied. When static, for owner customisation ritual, nothing can be contaminated or the mysterious poetic process shall be disturbed.

It is this highly personalised treatment that permits the ghost in the machine to haunt.

And how does this ethereal sensibility come into the steel, leather, rubber and plastics? The invisible component has a

123 *John Deere* custom Harley, built by Custom Ranch, Germany

124 Custom painted tank with American Indian imagery, Daytona, 1997

125

126

125 Harley-Davidson racing team,
Daytona, Florida, c.1920
© Harley-Davidson

126 Racing on wooden boards,
c.1920. Speeds of over
100mph could be achieved
during racing
© Harley-Davidson

127 1949 *Hydra Glide*.
Its classic front fender has
influenced a generation of
custom builders
© Harley-Davidson

heritage and can be envisioned through an awareness of shapes that Harleys have taken from a 1903 originator to the 1998 product. It is the shape, and the sound, of a Harley-Davidson motorcycle that bring the invisible into dramatic visible reality. Shapes can be seen, the sound can be heard, and both of these commandments sent forth by the factory are creatively altered by the rider, who, in essence, becomes a folk artist.

There are professionals who alter the stock appearance and sound, and they have discovered a commercial venture based upon personal adventure. They are not better or more deeply into it, but rather have simply carried their ritual to a different kind of garage – one with a parts counter and cash register. These business people have grown from doing it for themselves to doing it for others. If they have not evolved this way, their work will not appear authentic to the initiated. They may still make money and win bike shows, but they will not be among the chosen.

They are inspired as are the individual owners who customise. Both take their cues from the factory sculptures on wheels. In 1925, the Harley-Davidson teardrop petrol tank was inaugurated. This shape was restyled to appear even more sleek in 1936, when it was shortened and rounded more gracefully. On top of the tank, a teardrop-formed instrument cluster was mounted to complete the redesign. Under the seat on a 1936 EL, or Knucklehead as it was eventually known, was a wraparound oil tank, or Horseshoe oil tank.

There are industrial design objects that become more than the design itself. The Harley-Davidson teardrop petrol tank and Horseshoe oil tank are primary examples. Others would include the Gibson Les Paul guitar contour, Fender Stratocaster guitar cutaway, Colt single-action army pistol grip – objects designated for practicality but also 'look and feel' presentation. They are objects that have become known as evidence of things American and have attained universal appeal. Among other elements of

the Harley-Davidson motorcycle – such as the forty-five-degree V-twin engine, in existence since at least 1909, the front fender, as on the 1949 Hydra-Glide, and its related structural environment, and, of course, the very sound of the Harley – the gas tank and oil tank have shapes akin to the familiar ones noted herein that stir the imagination and create admirers and collectors. But only with the Harley-Davidson motorcycle come the customisers, the extenders of the stock look and feel. These folk artists are not changers, but rather modifiers.

The factory machines from Harley-Davidson receive personalised extensions, obvious and subtle variations on the historically evident Harley shapes. The idea is to keep the motorcycle looking, feeling and sounding like a Harley-Davidson, but imploding all this – not exploding it such that the bike no longer resembles a Harley – to meet personal folk demands. Factory custom fine art, function with style, transfers to rider custom folk art, function retained and style personalised.

127

III Vision

Willie G. Davidson took a courageous leap into the field of industrial design in 1971 with the FX 1200 Super Glide. The Super Glide received its moniker and custom appearance by joining the running gear and frame of the FL series to the sportier front end of the XL series. Big Twin and Sportster combined, indeed, but much more than the sum of its parent parts, the Super Glide set a standard that was greater than the 'F' from FL and the 'X' from XL.

The FX was a heavyweight Harley that changed the very nature of American motorcycling forever. Willie G. Davidson was, and still is, the leader when it comes to the sport

and aesthetic known as Harley-Davidson. Motorcycling is a sport, but it is also a way of being. As with designers such as Buckminster Fuller and Frank Lloyd Wright, Willie G. Davidson creates objects that in turn create a way of living. There are philosophies that rise out of Fuller's and Wright's materials, and there are followers of these designs that base entire life aesthetics upon them, but no single designer other than Willie G. Davidson, great grandson of one of the founders of the company, has produced such a vast aesthetic, held so close to the soul of so many. Willie G. knew that customising and personalising Harley-

Davidson motorcycles had for a long time been the very right and absolute privilege of Harley owners, and that this trend was radically increasing by the early 1970s. Willie G. believed it was the exact, right time for the Motor Company to take a leading role, and the '71 Super Glide did just that.

All of Willie G.'s creations do just that. His bikes tastefully herald the design heritage of Harley-Davidson while, at the same time, adjusting it forward into the present and on to the future. A typical example of his genius is the FXSTS, or Springer, reaching back to grab the present, pulling into the future. From Springer to Bad Boy and then Heritage Springer, Willie G. Davidson and his styling group have glanced at pre-1949 (when the telescopic fork was introduced) look and feel, notably with the 1948 model year, and then proceeded with vision to provide two-wheeled architecture that puts glorious nostalgia in touch with modern technology. The Springer front-end family, relatives of the Softail family, are factory customs quite unlike any

other and inspire their owners to exquisite customised detailing.

When Willie G. Davidson redesigned what originally was a customer's innovation and created the basic Softail, or FXST ('FX' combined with 'ST' for Softail), introduced in 1984, it appeared to be a Hardtail but was not. Shocks are under the bike, out of view, and not in the accepted rear-of-the-bike spot, creating and advancing an older look and feel replete with modern technological attributes. With its twenty-one-inch front wheel, the Softail was a startling approach to what a factory can put on its dealers' runways. Customisers could really take flight with this already radical presentation.

By virtue of this process, whereby the Motor Company product stays ahead of what it understands as its customers' expectations, providing motorcycles that are finely detailed in themselves, but at once always suggesting to the owner what possibilities might exist for his or her personalised version, the Harley-Davidson aesthetic starts with the bike and moves through the riders' lives.

129　Harley-Davidson FXSTS with springer forks, designed by Willie G. Davidson
© Harley-Davidson

Painted petrol tanks from America and Europe

138

140

139

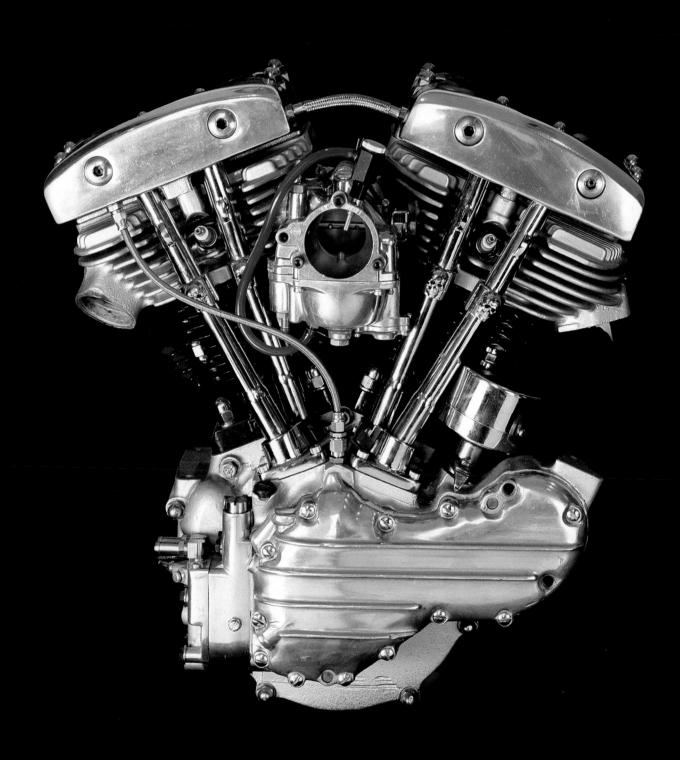

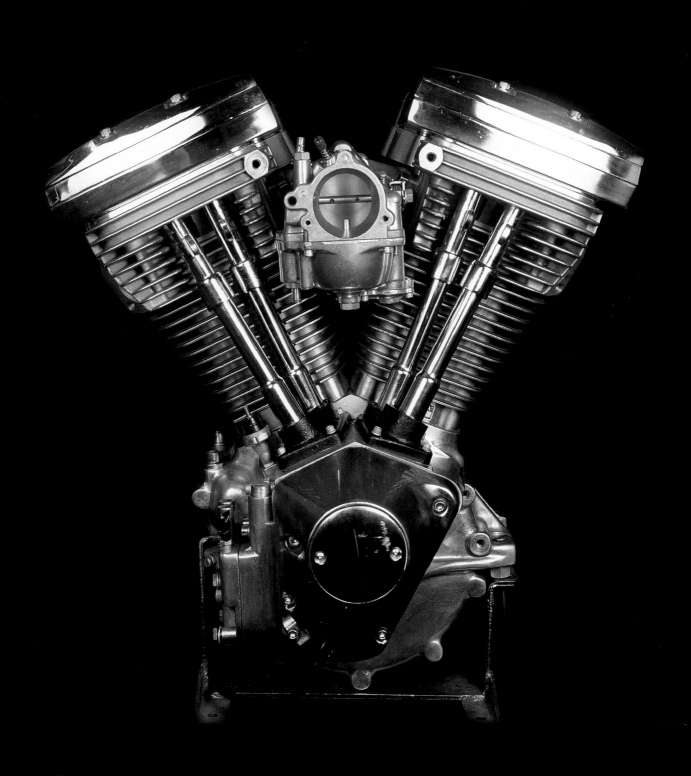

145

This movement from object to subject, bike to person, produces attributes that are artistic and philosophic. A creed with aesthetic definitions is shaped.

With the Harley-Davidson motorcycle as the altar, rituals of appearance, both in dress clothes and body skin art dressings, and even in ways of perceiving oneself that involve variations of individual freedom themes, become part of the stylised life. Diverse backgrounds are retained, as this is no melting pot, and a universal gathering of extreme individuals sharing all that the Harley means takes cultural shape. The Art of the Harley is, first and last, the motorcycle itself. However, if people could look like Harley-Davidsons they would, and they do by living the aesthetic such that this entire, mysterious process transcends philosophy and art, but includes it, and becomes a way of walking, talking, looking, thinking, feeling and, in essence, being.

When you customise a Harley-Davidson, you begin with a factory jewel that you polish according to your standard, and then you wear it, as it were, with all that you are as an individual. Such is the leadership of Willie G. Davidson, a man of great humility and vision, for he has a tactile and numinous understanding of Harley-Davidsons, and his presence is experienced in every throttle twist and exhaust blast.

The Art of the Harley is, ultimately, the greatest populist endeavour of this century. From the celluloid and print mediums to the blacktop curves, Harleys are taken on journeys both suggestive and literal, and have become the standard for non-standard approaches to life. The brand is an icon for making a difference.

145 Steve Morley's *Yellow Hammer* being ridden at Kent Custom Bike Show, 1997

146 Detail of *Flight DeVille* by Tank Ewsichek

147

147 Harley riders on Daytona beach at dawn

148 *Electra Glide* FLTR 95th anniversary edition
© Harley-Davidson

149 *Electra Glide* FLHT 95th anniversary edition
© Harley-Davidson

148

149

Harley riders at Sturgis

IV Journey

From the 1903 origin to this year of the ninety-fifth anniversary, 1998, the Harley-Davidson Motor Company has offered motorcycles of extraordinary durability and design.

Harley-Davidson motorcycles are one kind of art right out of the factory, then become another kind in the rider's garage, and then transform again into personal and cultural iconography. Mapping this route takes knowledge of things mechanical, education of matters related to design, and awareness of the wondrous ways human beings behave. But one does not have to make a map. One can just do all this, and let the map get outlined by authors such as myself. I have been involved with Harleys for many decades and, when writing about these beautiful motorcycles, always realise that riding them is what matters most. From riding comes an increased desire to under-stand what The Art of the Harley is all about, sure enough, but climbing back into the saddle after being at the typewriter is the journey. Essays are destinations; journeys are without goals, with just the rules of the road as limits. Please hear the roar of my exhaust note now that I am leaving this destination for the journey shared with all Harley riders. Please do study the Barbican exhibition in order to appreciate how the motorcycles have momentarily left the road for the exhibition hall.

Ultimately, the goal of the Harley-Davidson artistic experience is you in the saddle, sensing the custom motorcycle responding to your riding abilities. Then the union between man or woman and machine is as it should be: factory fine art and rider folk art have a singular intent, and this is to make the ride one of revelatory joy, lots of fun – and uniquely your own.

151 Harley riders' wedding, Sturgis, 1992

152 Harley riders on the road to Sturgis, South Dakota, beneath Bear Butte, a Sioux Indian holy mountain, 1990

The Bikes/
The Builders

Perhaps the most intriguing thing about all these bikes, these custom machines covered in bright hues and powered by roaring raucous V-twins, is the individuals who build them. Because behind every new fender shape or candy colour is a man or woman who thought it up. Each new light assembly or fender strut started out as an idea, became a sketch, then a mock-up in cardboard and eventually an idea expressed in metal. Just as fascinating as these wild machines are the individuals with the creative abilities and the personal drive to make it all happen.

These are the people who build motorcycles. Who take their own better ideas and craft them into two-wheeled reality. Most come from modest backgrounds, with no more than a high school or tech school education. Yet they get out of bed every day and create things that didn't exist before.

At a time when most products come off an automated assembly line, each custom motorcycle remains hand-built in the extreme. While we lament the passage of 'old world skills', the builders of custom bikes still fabricate sheet metal shapes with a hammer and a bag of sand, and inspire a younger generation to do the same.

The bikes are unique and beautiful. Each is made up of wonderful shapes and assembled with phenomenal attention to detail. More interesting than the bikes, however, are the individuals who conceive the ideas, fabricate the parts and ensure that it all comes together with that certain mechanical harmony and grace.

Tim Remus, 1997

123

The History of the Custom Harley

OWNER	Warrs H-D of London	MODEL	US Military

BIKE NAME	WLC	BUILDER	H-D

FRAME

Frame brand	H-D rigid		
Stock or modified	Stock		
Fork brand	H-D		
Swing-arm brand	None		
Front/Rear brake(s) brand	H-D drum		
Wheels brand	H-D	Size F/R	16" 16"
Tyres brand	Coker	Size F/R	5.00 x 16"

ENGINE

Year	1942				
Model	WLC Flathead	Bore	H-D	Stroke	H-D
Cases brand	H-D		Cylinders brand	H-D	
Cubic capacity	750 cc		Balanced	Yes	
Heads brand	H-D Ricardo type		Cam brand	H-D	
Carb brand	Linkert		Cam cover	H-D	
Air cleaner	H-D oil bath		Lifter blocks	H-D	
Exhaust pipes brand	H-D				
Ignition	H-D		Primary/derby covers	H-D	

TRANSMISSION

Speeds	3	Clutch	H-D	Modifications	None
Primary drive: belt or chain	Chain				
Final drive: belt or chain	Chain				

BODYWORK | ACCESSORIES | PAINT

Fender brand (front & rear)	H-D		
Custom body fabrication	None		
Petrol tank brand	H-D Fatbob	Bars	H-D
Seat brand/builder	H-D		
Paint colour	Khaki	Painter's name	H-D
Graphics	U.S. Army		

153

124

OWNER	Warrs H-D of London	MODEL	WLD

BIKE NAME	Bobber	BUILDER	H-D

FRAME

Frame brand	H-D		
Stock or modified	Stock		
Fork brand	H-D, modified		
Swing-arm brand	None		
Front/Rear brake(s) brand	H-D		
Wheels brand	Early alloy rims	Size F/R	16" 16"
Tyres brand	Coker	Size F/R	5.00 x 16"

ENGINE

Year	1942				
Model	WL	Bore	H-D	Stroke	H-D
Cases brand	H-D	Cylinders brand	H-D		
Cubic capacity	750 cc	Balanced	Yes		
Heads brand	Early Sifton	Cam brand	Sifton		
Carb brand	Bored Linkert				
Air cleaner	Mesh	Lifter blocks	H-D		
Exhaust pipes brand	Drag Dixon replicas				
Ignition	H-D	Primary/derby covers	H-D		

TRANSMISSION

Speeds	3	Clutch	H-D	Modifications	None
Primary drive: belt or chain	Chain				
Final drive: belt or chain	Chain				

BODYWORK | ACCESSORIES | PAINT

Fender brand (front & rear)	H-D, chopped		
Custom body fabrication	Period recreation		
Petrol tank brand	H-D, hand shift	Bars	H-D
Seat brand/builder	H-D		
Paint	Period recreation		
Graphics	H-D		

154

OWNER	Deutsches Zweirad and NSU Museum, Neckarsulm

BIKE NAME	Captain America	BUILDER	Reinhold Paukner

FRAME

Frame brand	Paughco Inc USA		
Stock or modified	Stretched 45°		
Fork brand	H-D Electra Glide 12" over		
Swing-arm brand	None		
Front/Rear brake(s) brand	H-D rear drum		
Wheels brand	H-D and aftermarket	Size F/R	21" 16"
Tyres size F/R	3.00 x 21" 130/90/16		

ENGINE

Year	1952 FL				
Model	Panhead	Bore	H-D	Stroke	H-D
Cases brand	H-D	Cylinders brand	H-D		
Cubic capacity	1200 cc	Balanced	H-D		
Heads brand	H-D	Cam brand	H-D		
Carb brand	Dell'Orto	Cam cover	Sifton		
Air cleaner	Custom aftermarket	Lifter blocks	H-D		
Exhaust pipes brand	Paughco upsweep fishtails				
Ignition	H-D	Primary/derby covers	H-D		

TRANSMISSION

Speeds	4	Clutch	H-D	Modifications	None
Primary drive: belt or chain	Chain				
Final drive: belt or chain	Chain				

BODYWORK | ACCESSORIES | PAINT

Fender brand (front & rear)	Rear aftermarket, modified		
Custom body fabrication	Paukis Harley-Davidson		
Petrol tank brand	Paughco, Mustang details	Bars	Apehangers
Paint colour	Red, white and blue		
Graphics	Stars and stripes		
Painter's name	Paukis H-D		

155

American Custom Harleys

OWNER | Arlen Ness

OWNER	Arlen Ness		
BIKE NAME	Two Bad	BUILDER	Arlen Ness

FRAME

Frame brand	Fabricated		
Stock or modified	Extremely custom		
Fork brand	Fabricated		
Swing-arm brand	None		
Front/Rear brake(s) brand	Hurst-Air Heart		
Wheels brand	Alum	Size F/R	19"
Tyres brand	Metzeler	Size F/R	19"

ENGINES

Year	Pre-Evo Iron-head Sportster engines		
Model	Two 900 cc engines with 1000 cc cylinders		
Cases brand	H-D	Cylinders brand	H-D
Cubic capacity	1000 cc each	Balanced & Ported	Yes
Heads brand	H-D	Cam brand	H-D
Carb brand	Weber's	Cam cover	Stock
Air cleaner	None	Lifter blocks	Stock
Exhaust pipes brand	Hand-fabricated		
Ignition	Magneto	Primary/derby covers	Gold-plated

TRANSMISSION

Speeds	4	Clutch	Stock	Modifications	Belt drive
Primary drive: belt or chain	Belt				
Final drive: belt or chain	Chain				

BODYWORK | ACCESSORIES | PAINT

Fender brand (front & rear)	Front: none; Rear: custom		
Custom body fabrication	Bob Munroe		
Petrol tank brand	Fabricated	Bars	Ness
Seat brand/builder	Danny Gray		
Paint colour	Purple	Painters	Arlen Ness and Jeff McCann
Graphics	Gold leaf		

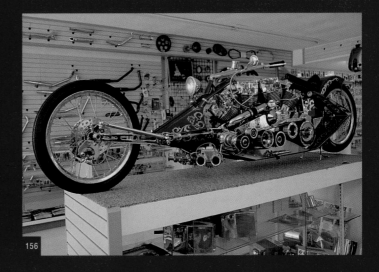

156

OWNER	Arlen Ness

BIKE NAME	Blown Shovel	BUILDER	Arlen Ness

FRAME

Frame brand	Arlen Ness		
Stock or modified	Cut & modified by J. Davis		
Fork brand	Showa		
Swing-arm brand	Arlen Ness		
Front/Rear brake(s) brand	Performance Machine		
Wheels brand	Front: spoked; Rear: fabricated	Size F/R	19"
Tyres brand	Rear: Continental dirt track	Size F/R	325/19 4.00 x 19"

ENGINE

Year	1979				
Model	Shovelhead	Bore	3⁷/₁₆"	Stroke	4¹/₄"
Cases brand	H-D			Cylinders brand	H-D
Cubic capacity	1300 cc			Balanced & Ported	Yes, by Carl's
Heads brand	H-D			Cam brand	Andrews
Carb brand	2-SU			Cam cover	H-D
Air cleaner	Velocity stacks			Lifter blocks	H-D
Exhaust pipes brand	Hand-made				
Ignition	Stock			Primary/derby covers	Special aluminium

TRANSMISSION

Speeds	4	Clutch	H-D	Modifications	H-D
Primary drive: belt or chain	Belt				
Final drive: belt or chain	Chain				

BODYWORK | ACCESSORIES | PAINT

Fender brand (front & rear)	Custom		
Custom body fabrication	Bob Munroe		
Petrol tank brand	Integrated in frame	Bars	Ness
Seat brand/builder	Danny Gray		
Paint colour	Brown	Painters	Arlen Ness and Jeff McCann
Graphics	Gold leaf		

157

OWNER	Arlen Ness

BIKE NAME	Ferrari Bike	BUILDER	Arlen Ness

FRAME

Frame brand	Ness built by Jim Davies		
Stock or modified	Hardtail		
Fork brand	Simons 'upside down' style		
Swing-arm brand	None		
Front/Rear brake(s) brand	Fabricated callipers one-off by Darrell Hayes		
Wheels brand	Fabricated	Size F/R	19" 16"
Tyres brand	Pirelli	Size F/R	19" rear 265/60/16

ENGINE

Year	1990				
Model	John Harman V-twin	Bore	4²/₅"	Stroke	4²/₅"
Cases brand	JH			Cylinders brand	H-D
Cubic capacity	2100 cc			Balanced & Ported	Yes
Heads brand	JH			Cam brand	Chane
Carb brand	Dell'Orto			Cam cover	H-D
Air cleaner	None			Lifter blocks	H-D
Exhaust pipes brand	Fabricated by Bob Munroe				
Ignition	Chane			Primary/derby covers	Ness

TRANSMISSION

Speeds	5	Clutch	H-D	Modifications	Belt drive
Primary drive: belt or chain	Belt				
Final drive: belt or chain	Belt				

BODYWORK | ACCESSORIES | PAINT

Fender brand (front & rear)	Fabricated by Craig Naff		
Custom body fabrication	Hand-fabricated		
Petrol tank brand	Custom	Oil tank brand	Custom
Seat brand/builder	Danny Gray	Lights	Custom
Paint colour	Special red from House of Kolor		
Graphics	Gold Leaf	Painter's name	Arlen Ness

158

OWNER	Arlen Ness		

BIKE NAME	Flamed Shovel	BUILDER	Arlen Ness

FRAME

Frame brand	Aftermarket Hardtail		
Stock or modified	Stock		
Fork brand	Paughco, springer		
Swing-arm brand	None		
Front/Rear brake(s) brand	No front brake		
Wheels brand	Spoked	Size F/R	21" 18"
Tyres brand	Metzeler	Size F/R	21" 18"

ENGINE

Year	1976				
Model	Shovelhead	Bore	$3^7/_{16}$"	Stroke	$4^1/_4$"
Cases brand	H-D		Cylinders brand	H-D	
Cubic capacity	1300 cc		Balanced & Ported	Yes	
Heads brand	H-D		Cam brand	H-D	
Carb brand	S & S, Super E		Cam cover	H-D	
Air cleaner	Ness		Lifter blocks	H-D	
Exhaust pipes brand	Fabricated by Bob Munroe				
Ignition	Dyna		Primary/derby covers	Ness	

TRANSMISSION

Speeds	4	Clutch	H-D	Modifications	None
Primary drive: belt or chain	Chain				
Final drive: belt or chain	Chain				

BODYWORK | ACCESSORIES | PAINT

Fender brand (front & rear)	Front: none; Rear: Ness, extended		
Custom body fabrication	Hand-fabricated		
Petrol tank brand	H-D, modified by Bob Munroe	Bars	Apehangers
Seat brand/builder	Danny Gray	Side covers	Bob Munroe
Paint colour	Red with flames		
Graphics	Flames	Painter's name	Ness

159

OWNER	Tank Ewsichek (Tank Tuff Cycles)	MODEL	FXR

BIKE NAME	Flight DeVille	BUILDER	Tank Ewsichek

FRAME

Frame brand	H-D FXR		
Stock or modified	Raked 35°, lowered 2"		
Fork brand	H-D, extended 2"		
Swing-arm brand	H-D		
Front/Rear brake(s) brand	H-D chromed callipers		
Wheels brand	Rev Tech	Size F/R	16" 16"
Tyres brand	Avon	Size F/R	130/16 140/16

ENGINE

Year	1995 rebuilt by Tom Pokorney				
Model	Evo	Bore	Stock $3^1/_2$"	Stroke	Stock $4^1/_4$"
Cases brand	S & S		Cylinders brand	H-D	
Cubic capacity	1300 cc		Balanced & Ported	Yes, by Tom Pokorey	
Heads brand	H-D		Cam brand	Andrews	
Carb brand	Dell'Orto		Cam cover	Arlen Ness	
Air cleaner	Dell'Orto		Lifter blocks	Arlen Ness	
Exhaust pipes brand	Tank				
Ignition	Dyna		Primary/derby covers	Ness	

TRANSMISSION

Speeds	5	Clutch	H-D	Modifications	Polished case
Primary drive: belt or chain	H-D chain				
Final drive: belt or chain	H-D chain				

BODYWORK | ACCESSORIES | PAINT

Fender brand (front & rear)	Indian style by Tank				
Custom body fabrication	Fabricated by Tank				
Petrol tank brand	Stretched	Oil tank brand	Stock FXR	Bars	Ness
Seat brand/builder	Donny Candis		Tail light	'59 Cadillac	
Paint colour	Pink				
Graphics	Green ellipses		Painter's name	Tank	

160

OWNER	Billy F. Gibbons	MODEL	Softail

BIKE NAME	HogZZilla	BUILDER	Bauder & Chapouris

FRAME

Frame brand	H-D
Stock or modified	Stock, lowered by 3"
Fork brand	H-D, lowered
Swing-arm brand	H-D, rear shocks are struts
Front/Rear brake(s) brand	H-D

Wheels brand	H-D	Size F/R	19" 16"
Tyres brand		Size F/R	19" 16"

ENGINE

Year	1991				
Model	Evo	Bore	3¹⁄₂"	Stroke	4¹⁄₄"

Cases brand	H-D	Cylinders brand	H-D
Cubic capacity	1300 cc	Balanced & Ported	No
Heads brand	H-D	Cam brand	H-D
Carb brand	Keihin	Cam cover	H-D
Air cleaner	Under chrome spear	Lifter blocks	H-D

Exhaust pipes brand	Custom, hand-formed

Ignition	H-D	Primary/derby covers	H-D

TRANSMISSION

Speeds	5	Clutch	Stock
Primary drive: belt or chain		H-D chain	
Final drive: belt or chain		H-D belt	

BODYWORK ACCESSORIES PAINT

Fender brand (front & rear)	Hand-fabricated by Steve Davis		
Custom body fabrication	Steve Davis		

Petrol tank brand	Fabricated	Oil tank brand	H-D	Bars	H-D

Seat brand/builder	Ron Magus	Lights	Fabricated
Paint colour	Candy eggplant from House of Kolor		
Graphics	None	Painters	John Carambia and Tim Beard

161

OWNER	Cyril Huze Custom	MODEL	FL

BIKE NAME	Miami Nice	BUILDER	Cyril Huze

FRAME

Frame brand	H-D FLH
Stock or modified	Raked 39° and moulded
Fork brand	H-D Wide glide, lowered by 2"
Swing-arm brand	H-D, modified by Cyril Huze
Front/Rear brake(s) brand	JayBrake 4-piston

Wheels brand	Chrome spoked	Size F/R	16" 16"
Tyres brand	Avon	Size F/R	130/90/16 140/90/16

ENGINE

Year	1977 rebuilt 1996				
Model	Shovelhead rebuilt by Sachs	Bore	3⁷⁄₁₆"	Stroke	4¹⁄₄"

Cases brand	H-D	Cylinders brand	H-D
Cubic capacity	1300 cc	Balanced & Ported	
Heads brand	Polished & painted	Cam brand	Crane
Carb brand	S & S Shorty	Cam cover	H-D
Air cleaner	Cyril Huze	Lifter blocks	H-D

Exhaust pipes brand	Cyril Huze, engraved

Ignition	Dyna	Primary/derby covers	H-D engraved

TRANSMISSION

Speeds	5	Clutch	Custom
Primary drive: belt or chain		H-D chain	
Final drive: belt or chain		H-D chain	

BODYWORK ACCESSORIES PAINT

Fender brand (front & rear)	Custom built by Cyril Huze		
Custom body fabrication	Teddy Brak & Glen Kotsman		

Petrol tank brand	Stretched	Oil tank brand	CCI, extended/engraved

Seat brand/builder	Phipps/Schreck	Lights	Custom Cyril Huze
Paint colour	Custom mix of blue/purple Florida pastels, PPG		
Graphics	Cyril Huze & Brigette Le Jeloux	Painter's name	C. Cruz

162

OWNER	Drag Specialties	MODEL	Dyna Glide

BUILDER	Dave Perewitz

FRAME

Frame brand	H-D Dyna Glide modified by Cycle Fab		
Stock or modified	Stretched 1½", raked 37°		
Fork brand	H-D with progressive springs		
Swing-arm brand	H-D, modified by Cycle Fab		
Front/Rear brake(s) brand	GMA, Russell brake lines		
Wheels brand	Boyds Daytona	Size F/R	19" 16"
Tyres brand	Avon	Size F/R	90/90/19 140/80/16

ENGINE

Year	1994				
Model	Evo		Bore	3½"	Stroke	4¼"
Cases brand	H-D		Cylinders brand	H-D	
Cubic capacity	800 cc		Balanced & Ported	Yes	
Heads brand	Edelbrock		Cam brand	Stock	
Carb brand	Quiksilver		Cam cover	Arlen Ness	
Air cleaner	Quiksilver		Lifter blocks	Arlen Ness	
Exhaust pipes brand	Python 3		Push rod tubes	Arlen Ness	
Ignition	Crane		Primary/derby covers	Drag Specialties	

TRANSMISSION

Speeds	5	Clutch	Pro 1 Hydraulic
Primary drive: belt or chain	H-D chain		
Final drive: belt or chain	H-D belt		

BODYWORK ACCESSORIES PAINT

Fender brand (front & rear)	Cycle Fab		
Custom body fabrication	Dave Perewitz & Drag Specialties		
Petrol tank brand	Stretched by Cycle Fab	Oil tank brand	H-D
Seat brand/builder	Drag Specialties	Lights	Drag Specialties
Paint colour	Shimrin pearls and Kandies, House of Kolor		
Graphics	Nancy Brooks, Brooks Sign	Painter's name	Dave Perewitz

163

OWNER	Bobby Sullivan	MODEL	Softail

BIKE NAME	Purple Roadster	BUILDER	Dave Perewitz

FRAME

Frame brand	Custom Chrome		
Stock or modified	Stretched 2", raked 36°, lowered 2"		
Fork brand	Boyds billet aluminium, 41mm tubes		
Swing-arm brand	Custom Chrome, torsion bar suspension		
Front/Rear brake(s) brand	Arlen Ness		
Wheels brand	Perewitz/Sullivan, billet aluminium	Size F/R	17" 17"
Tyres brand	Avon	Size F/R	Rear 190/17

ENGINE

Year	1996, built from aftermarket parts				
Model	V-twin		Bore	3½"	Stroke	4⅝"
Cases brand	Delkron		Cylinders brand	H-D/Edelbrock heads	
Cubic capacity	1500 cc		Balanced & Ported	Yes	
Heads brand	Edelbrock		Cam brand	Crane	
Carb brand	Edelbrock, Quiksilver		Cam cover	Billet alum. Ness	
Air cleaner	Cycle Fab		Lifter blocks	Ness	
Exhaust pipes brand	Bub		Push rod tubes	Arlen Ness	
Ignition	Crane Hi-4		Primary/derby covers	Billet alum. Ness	

TRANSMISSION

Speeds	5, Rev Tech	Clutch	H-D	Modifications	Polished case
Primary drive: belt or chain	H-D chain				
Final drive: belt or chain	H-D belt				

BODYWORK ACCESSORIES PAINT

Fender brand (front & rear)	Jesse James		
Custom body fabrication	Cycle Fab		
Petrol tank brand	Fabricated by Cycle Fab		
Seat brand/builder	Danny Gray	Tail light	Cycle Fab
Paint colour	Kandy Magenta, House of Kolor		
Graphics	Nancy Brooks, Brooks Sign	Painter's name	Cycle Fab

164

OWNER	Drag Specialties		MODEL	FXSTC

BUILDER	Don Hotop

FRAME

Frame brand	H-D FXSTC modified by Hotop		
Stock or modified	Stretched 1½", raked 37°		
Fork brand	H-D with progressive springs		
Swing-arm brand	H-D, modified by Hotop		
Front/Rear brake(s) brand	GMA, with Russell lines		
Wheels brand	Performance Machine Viper	Size F/R	19" 16"
Tyres brand	Avon	Size F/R	90/90/19 140/80/16

ENGINE

Year	1993					
Model	Evo		Bore	3½"	Stroke	4½"
Cases brand	H-D		Cylinders brand	H-D		
Cubic capacity	800 cc		Balanced & Ported	Yes		
Heads brand	Edelbrock		Cam brand	Crane		
Carb brand	McKay's		Cam cover	Arlen Ness		
Air cleaner	Don Hotop		Lifter blocks	Arlen Ness		
Exhaust pipes brand	Cycle Shack		Push rod tubes	Arlen Ness		
Ignition	Crane	Primary/derby covers	Drag Specialties/Don Hotop			

TRANSMISSION

Speeds	5	Clutch	Barnett clutch
Primary drive: belt or chain	H-D chain		
Final drive: belt or chain	H-D belt		

BODYWORK | ACCESSORIES | PAINT

Fender brand (front & rear)	Drag Specialties		
Custom body fabrication	Don Hotop & Drag Specialties		
Petrol tank brand	Hotop	Oil tank brand	Drag Specialties
Seat brand/builder	Drag Specialties	Lights	Drag Specialties
Paint colour	Urethane paint (blue blood red) from House of Kolor		
Graphics	Nancy Brooks, Brooks Sign	Painter's name	Dave Perewitz

165

OWNER	Jill Bell		MODEL	Softail

BIKE NAME	Santa Fe		BUILDER	Dave Bell

FRAME

Frame brand	H-D		
Stock or modified	Lowered by 1½" and moulded		
Fork brand	H-D		
Swing-arm brand	H-D with progressive shocks		
Front/Rear brake(s) brand	JB		
Wheels brand	H-D	Size F/R	16" 16"
Tyres brand	Dunlop	Size F/R	16" 16"

ENGINE

Year	1996					
Model	Softail		Bore	3⅝"	Stroke	4½"
Cases brand	Delkron		Cylinders brand	Sputle		
Cubic capacity	1600 cc		Balanced & Ported	Yes		
Heads brand	Edelbrock		Cam brand	Crane, Fireball		
Carb brand	S & S					
Air cleaner	S & S with stretched cover					
Exhaust pipes brand	Sampson					
Ignition	Dyna		Primary/derby covers	H-D		

TRANSMISSION

Speeds	5	Modifications	None
Primary drive: belt or chain	H-D chain		
Final drive: belt or chain	H-D belt		

BODYWORK | ACCESSORIES | PAINT

Fender brand (front & rear)	Street Sweeper		
Custom body fabrication and paint work	Paul Erpenbeck		
Petrol tank brand	H-D stretched		
Seat brand/builder	Capitol H-D	Bars	Beach bars
Paint colour	Beige, creme, coral and turquoise		
Graphics	Paul Erpenbeck	Chrome work	Browns Plating

166

OWNER	Bob Dron	MODEL	FLSTC

BIKE NAME	Roadster Royale	BUILDER	Bob Dron Design Center

FRAME

Frame brand	Softail style, built by Daytec
Stock or modified	Raked 38°
Fork brand	H-D/Buell
Swing-arm brand	Daytec
Front/Rear brake(s) brand	Buell

Wheels brand	Buell	Size F/R	17" 17"
Tyres brand	Dunlop	Size F/R	120/17 170/17

ENGINE

Year	1993, rebuilt by Bob Dron Harley-Davidson				
Model	Evo		Bore	$3^1/_2$"	Stroke	$4^1/_4$"

Cases brand	H-D	Cylinders brand	H-D

Cubic capacity	1300 cc	Balanced	Yes, by Bob Dron Design Center

Heads brand	Edelbrock	Cam brand	Crane 316B
Carb brand	Edelbrock Quiksilver	Cam cover	H-D
Air cleaner	Stock with rivets	Lifter blocks	H-D

Exhaust pipes brand	Vance & Hines
Ignition	Compu-Fire

TRANSMISSION

Speeds	5	Clutch	H-D	Modifications	None
Primary drive: belt or chain		H-D chain			
Final drive: belt or chain		H-D belt			

BODYWORK | ACCESSORIES | PAINT

Fender brand (front & rear)	Bob Dron Design Center
Custom body fabrication	Steve Moal

Petrol tank brand	FXRS with covers	Bars	883 H-D/H-D grips
Seat brand/builder	You call that a seat?	Lights	H-D/Bob Dron

Paint colour	None (polished aluminium, bare metal)

Graphics	None	Chroming	Sherm's

167

OWNER	Nace Panzica – CCI	MODEL	FXSTS

BUILDER	Rick Doss

FRAME

Frame brand	H-D
Stock or modified	Lowered by 2"
Fork brand	H-D
Swing-arm brand	RDI one of a kind
Front/Rear brake(s) brand	Rev Tech, chrome

Wheels brand	RDI	Size F/R	21" 18"
Tyres brand	Avon	Size F/R	3.00 x 21" 140/18

ENGINE

Year	1989				
Model	Evo		Bore	$3^1/_2$"	Stroke	$4^1/_4$"

Cases brand	H-D	Cylinders brand	H-D

Cubic capacity	1300 cc	Balanced	Yes

Heads brand	Rev Tech	Cam brand	Rev Tech 40
Carb brand	Rev Tech		
Air cleaner	Rev Tech RDI		

Exhaust pipes brand	RDI		
Ignition	Rev Tech	Primary/derby covers	H-D

TRANSMISSION

Speeds	5	Modifications	Rev Tech gears
Primary drive: belt or chain		H-D chain	
Final drive: belt or chain		H-D belt	

BODYWORK | ACCESSORIES | PAINT

Fender brand (front & rear)	Hand-made RDI
Custom body fabrication	RDI
Petrol tank brand	RDI, stretched

Seat brand/builder	Danny Gray	Bars	CCI by RDI
Paint colour	Shimmer yellow pearl	Painter's name	Tommy Fowler
Graphics	Eddie Meeks	Chrome work	Browns Plating

168

OWNER	Nace Panzica – CCI	MODEL	FXSTC

BIKE NAME	Eclipse	BUILDER	Rick Doss

FRAME

Frame brand	H-D/RDI		
Stock or modified	Lowered by 2", rake/fork angle – 1"		
Fork brand	H-D/RDI cut by $1^{1}/_{2}$"		
Swing-arm brand	Progressive, 1" over stock		
Front/Rear brake(s) brand	Rev Tech, chrome		
Wheels brand	RDI	Size F/R	21" 16"
Tyres brand	Avon	Size F/R	3.00 x 21" 140/16

ENGINE

Year	1992				
Model	Evo		Bore	$3^{1}/_{2}$"	Stroke	$4^{1}/_{4}$"
Cases brand	STD	Cylinders brand	H-D		
Cubic capacity	1300 cc	Balanced & Ported	Yes		
Heads brand	Rev Tech	Cam brand	Rev Tech 40		
Carb brand	Rev Tech				
Air cleaner	RDI				
Exhaust pipes brand	RDI				
Ignition	Rev Tech	Primary/derby covers	H-D		

TRANSMISSION

Speeds	5	Modifications	Rev Tech gears
Primary drive: belt or chain	H-D chain		
Final drive: belt or chain	H-D belt		

BODYWORK ACCESSORIES° PAINT

Fender brand (front & rear)	Hand-made RDI		
Custom body fabrication	RDI		
Petrol tank brand	RDI, stretched/frenched caps		
Seat brand/builder	Danny Gray	Bars	CCI by RDI
Paint colour	Black	Painter's name	Tommy Fowler
Graphics	Stainless Steel Emblems	Chrome work	Browns Plating

169

OWNER	Bob McKay	MODEL	Bar Hopper

BUILDER	Bob McKay		

FRAME

Frame brand	Chopper Guys		
Stock or modified	Stretched $1^{3}/_{4}$", rake/fork angle – 30°		
Fork brand	Ness		
Swing-arm brand	None (rigid, Hardtail)		
Front/Rear brake(s) brand	Rev Tech CCI		
Wheels brand	Ness	Size F/R	21" 16"
Tyres brand	Avon	Size F/R	90/90/21 200/60/16

ENGINE

Year	1997				
Model	Evo		Bore	$3^{5}/_{8}$"	Stroke	$4^{5}/_{8}$"
Cases brand	T.P. Engineering	Cylinders brand	S & S		
Cubic capacity	960 cc	Balanced & Ported	Yes		
Heads brand	Edenbruch	Cam brand	Crane		
Carb brand	Mikuni				
Air cleaner	Mikuni				
Exhaust pipes brand	McKay's Sampson				
Ignition	Crane Hi-4	Primary/derby covers	Ness		

TRANSMISSION

Speeds	5	Modifications	Full Andrews close ratio
Primary drive: belt or chain	H-D chain		
Final drive: belt or chain	H-D belt		

BODYWORK ACCESSORIES PAINT

Fender brand (front & rear)	Front: none; Rear: Jesse James		
Custom body fabrication	McKay's		
Petrol tank brand	Ness – hidden mounts (rubber isolator)		
Seat brand/builder	Danny Gray	Bars	Ness
Paint colour	Chevy red	Painter's name	Bob McKay
Graphics	None	Chrome work	Plating House

170

133

OWNER	Harley-Davidson UK	MODEL	FLSTS

BIKE NAME	Heritage Springer	BUILDER	H-D Motor Company

FRAME

Frame brand	H-D, tubular cradle		
Stock or modified	Stock		
Fork brand	Chrome 'Springer' style		
Swing-arm brand	H-D, tubular mild steel		
Front/Rear brake(s) brand	H-D disc		
Wheels brand	H-D	Size F/R	16" 16"
Tyres brand	Wide whitewall	Size F/R	16"/16"

ENGINE

Year	1998				
Model	Evolution	Bore	$3^1/_2$"	Stroke	$4^1/_4$"
Cases brand	H-D		Cylinders brand	H-D	
Cubic capacity	1340 cc		Balanced	H-D	
Heads brand	H-D		Cam brand	H-D	
Carb brand	H-D		Cam covers	H-D	
Air cleaner	H-D		Lifter blocks	H-D	
Exhaust pipes brand	H-D crossover dual with fishtail silencers				
Ignition	H-D		Primary/derby covers	H-D	

TRANSMISSION

Speeds	5	Clutch	H-D	Modifications	None
Primary drive: belt or chain	Chain				
Final drive: belt or chain	Belt				

BODYWORK   ACCESSORIES   PAINT

Fender brand (front & rear)	H-D		
Tail light brand/style	Tombstone		
Petrol tank brand	H-D with panel trim	Bars	FLH style
Seat brand/builder	Factory custom		
Paint colour	95th Anniversary colours		
Graphics	H-D	Painter's name	H-D

171

134

European Custom Harleys

OWNER	Battistinis	MODEL	FXR

BIKE NAME	The FXR-SS	BUILDER	Jeff Duval

FRAME

Frame brand	1993 FXR Custom built by Batt Gang/Cobra				
Stock or modified	Stretched 5", Raked 40°				
Fork brand	Prototypes, Ness Yokes, built by Battistinis/G. Duffy				
Swing-arm brand	Ness Twin Rail	Shocks	Ness Billet		
Front/Rear brake(s) brand	PM 13" Viper Disc x 2 PM Calliper				
Wheels brand	Ness/SS spokes/Akfront	Size F/R	2.50 x 19" 4.25 x 16"		
Tyres brand	Metzeler	Size F/R	100/90/19 150/60/18		

ENGINE

Year	1992 rebuilt at Carl's Speed Shop				
Model	Evo	Bore	3⁵⁄₈"	Stroke	4¹⁄₄"
Cases brand	S & S		Cylinders brand	C.S.S.	
Cubic capacity	1440 cc		Balanced	Stock	
Heads brand	C.S.S.		Cam brand	C.S.S. CM580	
Carb brand	S & S		Cam cover	Ness	
Air cleaner	Velo Stack		Lifter blocks	Stock	
Exhaust pipes and silencers brand	Batt Gang Custom				
Ignition	Crane Single Fire Hi-4		Primary/derby covers	Ness	

TRANSMISSION

Speeds	5	Clutch	Barnett	Modifications	Polished
Primary drive: belt or chain	Chain				
Final drive: belt or chain	Belt				

BODYWORK   ACCESSORIES   PAINT

Fender brand (front & rear)	Batt Gang Custom			
Petrol tank brand	Ness Custom			
Bars	Drag Ness, Ness Billet Satin grips			
Seat brand/builder	Dave Batchelar	Lights	Ness/Batt Gang	
Paint colour	Team Lotus Racing	Painter's name	Terry Spencer	
Graphics	Terry Spencer	Chroming	London Chroming	

172

OWNER	Battistinis	MODEL	Softail

BIKE NAME	The Cruiser	BUILDER	Jeff Duval

FRAME

Frame brand	Sumax Rubbermount modified by Battistinis				
Stock or modified	Stretched 6", raked 40°				
Fork brand	Leading axle custom, 2" under, Ness narrowglide yokes				
Swing-arm brand	Cobra Engineering		Shocks	Progressive	
Front/Rear brake(s) brand	Dual PM 125 x 4R/PM 125 x 4R				
Wheels brand	PM hub/Akfront rim	Size F/R	1.85 x 21" 5.5 x 18"		
Tyres brand	Metzeler	Size F/R	80/90/21 180/55/18		

ENGINE

Year	1994 rebuilt by Rich Products/Ness				
Model	Evo				
Cases brand	Delkron Custom		Cylinders brand	Axtell	
Cubic capacity	2050 cc		Balanced	Rich Products	
Heads brand	Re-worked STD		Cam brand	4 x Delkron Custom	
Carb brand	S & S Super D		Cam covers	Ness	
Air cleaner	Ness scalloped		Lifter blocks	H-D	
Exhaust pipes brand	Custom stainless, Kalashnikov silencers				
Ignition	Crane Hi-4		Primary/derby covers	Ness	

TRANSMISSION

Speeds	5	Clutch	Barnet	Modifications	Polished
Primary drive: belt or chain	Chain				
Final drive: belt or chain	O-ring chain				

BODYWORK   ACCESSORIES   PAINT

Fender brand (front & rear)	Custom aluminium/'Cruiser Series'			
Petrol tank brand	'Cruiser Series'			
Bars	Drag Ness, Ness flamed grips			
Seat brand/builder	Dave Batchelar	Lights	Headwinds/Ness	
Paint colour	Mediterranean candy blue	Painter's name	Jeff McCann	
Graphics	Fire red flames & shadows	Chroming	London Chroming	

173

OWNER	Battistinis		MODEL	Softail

BIKE NAME	Paint it Black		BUILDER	Rikki Battistini

FRAME

Frame brand	H-D Softail, lowered 1"		
Stock or modified	Stretched 5", raked 35°		
Fork brand	Battistinis custom, 2" over, Ness radius yokes		
Swing-arm brand	H-D 1" Stretch	Shocks	Progressive chromed
Front/Rear brake(s) brand	Dual Ness/PM 4 piston/Ness/PM 4 piston		
Wheels brand	Ness hub/Akront rim	Size F/R	1.85 x 21" 5.5 x 18"
Tyres brand	Metzeler	Size F/R	80/90/21 180/55/18

ENGINE

Year	1997 rebuilt by Battistinis				
Model	S & S/Patrick Billet	Bore	$3^5/_8$"	Stroke	$4^1/_4$"
Cases brand	S & S	Cylinders brand	Patrick Billet		
Cubic capacity	1475 cc	Balanced	Ness		
Heads brand	Patrick Billet	Cam brand	Crane Fireball		
Carb brand	S & S Super E	Cam covers	Ness		
Air cleaner	Ness Radius	Lifter blocks	H-D		
Exhaust pipes brand	Ness by Bub, mufflers by Bub				
Ignition	Crane Hi-4	Primary/derby covers	Ness		

TRANSMISSION

Speeds	5	Clutch	Barnett	Modifications	Polished
Primary drive: belt or chain	Chain				
Final drive: belt or chain	O-ring chain				

BODYWORK | ACCESSORIES | PAINT

Fender brand (front & rear)	Battistinis custom aluminium		
Petrol tank brand	'Cruiser Series'		
Bars	Battistinis, 4" risers, Ness grips		
Seat brand/builder	Danny Gray	Lights	Ness/Ness Cateye
Paint colour	Black & deep grey, Met. PPG	Painter's name	Jeff McCann
Graphics	Japanese Leaf	Chroming	London Chroming

174

OWNER	Richard Taylor		MODEL	2 Litre Blower

BIKE NAME	Blower		BUILDER	Richard Taylor

FRAME

Frame brand	P & D Custom		
Stock or modified	Stretched, raked 35°, moulded & lowered		
Fork brand	GSXR 1100, cut		
Swing-arm brand	Hand-made	Shocks	Modified stock units
Front/Rear brake(s) brand	Harrison 4 x 6 pistons/2 x 6 pistons		
Wheels brand	Akront	Size F/R	3.00 x 19" 5.75 x 18"
Tyres brand	Metzeler	Size F/R	110/90/19 180/55/18

ENGINE

Year	1980s rebuilt by R. J. Taylor/Matts Engineering				
Model	John Harman	Bore	$4^3/_4$"	Stroke	Stock 1200
Cases brand	Harman	Cylinders brand	Harman		
Cubic capacity	2000 cc	Balanced & Ported	Yes		
Heads brand	Harman	Cam brand	Andrews		
Carb brand	Dell'Orto DHLA 45 (x2)	Cam specs	High lift short dur.		
Air cleaner	K & N	Lifter blocks	H-D		
Exhaust pipes brand	Hand-made s/s				
Ignition	Crane Hi-4	Primary/derby covers	H-D/Hand-made		

TRANSMISSION

Speeds	5	Clutch	H-D	Modifications	Reversed gear linkage
Primary drive: belt or chain	Chain				
Final drive: belt or chain	Regina chain, sprockets 24/48				

BODYWORK | ACCESSORIES | PAINT

Fender brand (front & rear)	Handmade by P & D		
Custom body fabrication	R. J. Taylor + P & D		
Petrol tank brand	H-D Sportster/Mod	Bars	P & D
Seat brand/builder	P & D	Lights	Frenched Cats eyes (rear)
Paint colour	Cherry	Painter's name	Matt the Painter
Graphics	Cherry splashes	Chroming	London Chroming

175

OWNER	Andrew Peters	MODEL	1994 Jeez Louise!

BIKE NAME	Eleganté	BUILDER	Andrew Peters

FRAME

Frame brand	Jeez Louise
Stock or modified	One-off by Jeez Louise, stretched and raked
Fork brand	Jeez Louise, one-off, 4" over

Swing-arm brand	Jeez Louise	Shocks	H-D FLH

Front/Rear brake(s) brand	Billet polished 6 piston/4 piston		

Wheels brand	Jeez Louise	Size F/R	21" 15"

Tyres brand	Avon/Pirelli	Size F/R	3.00 x 21" 1.85/15

ENGINE

Year	1974 rebuilt by Jeez Louise				
Model	Shovel	Bore	Stock	Stroke	Stock
Cases brand	H-D		Cylinders brand	H-D	
Cubic capacity	1200 cc		Balanced & Ported	Yes, by JL	
Heads brand	H-D		Cam brand	H-D	
Carb brand	SU		Cam specs	Stock	
Air cleaner	Velocity stacks Jeez Louise		Lifter blocks	H-D	
Exhaust pipes brand	Jeez Louise				
Ignition	Crane Single Fire		Primary/derby covers	H-D	

TRANSMISSION

Speeds	5	Clutch	H-D	Modifications	Polished case

Primary drive: belt or chain	H-D chain

Final drive: belt or chain	Jeez Louise chain, sprockets 51/23

BODYWORK | ACCESSORIES | PAINT

Fender brand (front & rear)	Jeez Louise fibreglass		
Custom body fabrication	Jeez Louise		
Petrol tank brand	Jeez Louise	Bars	Jeez Louise stainless
Seat brand/builder	Connolly hide	Lights	Jeez Louise
Paint colour	Green	Painters	Jeez Louise & Cockney Dave
Graphics	Jeez Louise	Chroming	All stainless steel

176

OWNER	Steve Morley ('Big Steve')	MODEL	FXR

BIKE NAME	Yellow Hammer	BUILDER	Steve Morley

FRAME

Frame brand	FXR
Stock or modified	Modified by Big Steve
Fork brand	GSX-R (Suzuki), extended by 3", yokes by Big Steve & Bob

Swing-arm brand	Big Steve & Notts Customs	Shocks	Progressive

Front/Rear brake(s) brand	Modified billet polished 6/4 x 2/Pm discs		

Wheels brand	Rev Tech	Size F/R	16" 16"

Tyres brand	Dunlop	Size F/R	5.00 x 16"

ENGINE

Year	1991 rebuilt by Jimmy Doom, Flowtech				
Model	Big Twin	Bore	Stock	Stroke	Stock
Cases brand	H-D		Cylinders brand	H-D	
Cubic capacity	1340 cc				
Heads brand	4-Angle valve seats		Cam brand	Modified Andrews EV3	
Carb brand	Carl's Speed Shop 'Typhoon'				
Air cleaner	Carl's Speed Shop		Lifter blocks	HeadQuarters	
Exhaust pipes brand	Big Steve & Grand Fabrication				
Ignition	Dyna single-fire, competition advance				

TRANSMISSION

Speeds	5	Clutch	Stock	Modifications	Stock

Primary drive: belt or chain	H-D chain, chrome cover

Final drive: belt or chain	Belt

BODYWORK | ACCESSORIES | PAINT

Fender brand (front & rear)	Big Steve & Steve Gagg		
Petrol tank brand	Big Steve & Steve Gagg		
Bars	Big Steve & Bob		
Seat brand/builder	Big Steve	Lights	Big Steve & Bob (rear, cateye)
Paint colour	Yellow, yellow pearl & purple, 2-pack (The Paint Studio)		
Paint & Graphics	Big Steve & Steve Lowe	Chroming	London Chroming

177

OWNER	George Savage	MODEL	1993 Ultra Classic Electra Glide

BIKE NAME	Suttle	BUILDER	George Savage

FRAME

Frame brand	FLH			
Stock or modified	Stock			
Fork brand	Telescopic			
Swing-arm brand	FLH		Shocks	Stock
Front/Rear brake(s) brand	Twin disc/disc			
Wheels brand	Cast 10 spoke	Size F/R	16" 16"	
Tyres brand	Dunlop Tourism Elite	Size F/R	16" 16"	

ENGINE

Year	1993				
Model	Evo	Bore	Stock	Stroke	Stock
Cases brand	H-D		Cylinders brand	H-D	
Cubic capacity	1340 cc				
Heads brand	H-D		Cam brand	H-D	
Carb brand	H-D		Cam specs	H-D	
Air cleaner	H-D Circular		Lifter blocks	H-D	
Exhaust pipes brand	Two-into-one				
Ignition	Electronic				

TRANSMISSION

Speeds	5	Clutch	Stock	Modifications	Stock
Primary drive: belt or chain	Chain				
Final drive: belt or chain	Belt				

BODYWORK | ACCESSORIES | PAINT

Fender brand (front & rear)	Stock FLHT			
Custom body fabrication	None			
Petrol tank brand	Fatbob		Bars	Dresser
Seat brand/builder	Dual	Lights	6" sealed beam front/H-D	
Paint colour	Black			
Paint & Graphics	H-D		Chroming	H-D

178

OWNER	Nicolas Chauvin	MODEL	H-D 1980

BIKE NAME	Tribute to Stevie Ray Vaughan	BUILDER	N. Chauvin

FRAME

Frame brand	Nicolas Chauvin			
Stock or modified	Stretched, raked & lowered			
Fork brand	Upside-down Kayaba			
Swing-arm brand	Stretched 10cm		Shocks	Yamaha FZX (rigid)
Front/Rear brake(s) brand	Nissin 4 pistons/double pistons			
Wheels brand	Suzuki GSXR/Wild	Size F/R	17" 15"	
Tyres brand	Goodyear Agnatred	Size F/R	120/70/17 205/70/15	

ENGINE

Year	1980				
Model	Shovelhead	Bore	Stock	Stroke	Stock
Cases brand	Delkron		Cylinders brand	H-D	
Cubic capacity	1340 cc		Balanced	Yes	
Heads brand	Stock		Cam brand	Rivera 'Macho'	
Carb brand	Dell'Orto		Cam covers	Morris	
Air cleaner	Nicolas Chauvin		Lifter blocks	Andrews	
Exhaust pipes & silencers brand	Nicolas Chauvin				
Ignition	Morris M5 + MSF dual plugs		Primary/derby covers	Chauvin	

TRANSMISSION

Speeds	4	Clutch	Barnett Kevlar	Modifications	Remoce gear box
Primary drive: belt or chain	Karata 3' belt with cover				
Final drive: belt or chain	Chain				

BODYWORK | ACCESSORIES | PAINT

Fender brand (front & rear)	Suzuki GSXR/Nicolas Chauvin			
Custom body fabrication	Nicolas Chauvin			
Petrol tank brand	Nicolas Chauvin		Bars	Nicolas Chauvin
Seat brand/builder	Nicolas Chauvin	Lights	Bates/Nicolas Chauvin	
Paint colour	Fluorescent Candy		Painter's name	Nicolas Chauvin
Graphics	Nicolas Chauvin		Chroming	Nicolas Chauvin

179

OWNER	Danny Franssen		MODEL	Evo

BIKE NAME	Harley Trike		BUILDER	Danny Franssen

FRAME

Frame brand	Designed by owner, manufactured by A. Johansson
Stock or modified	1" downtubes, raked 50°
Fork brand	Home-made 10" overstock

Swing-arm brand	None	Shocks	None/Hardtail

Rear brake brand	Billet CNC		

Wheels brand	Boyd's/Colorado custom	Size F/R	21"/15" x 12½"

Tyres brand	Avon/Yokohama	Size F/R	3.00 x 21" 345/35/15

ENGINE

Year	1996			

Model	Evo	Bore	3⅝"	Stroke	4½"

Cases brand	H-D	Cylinders brand	H-D

Cubic capacity	1500 cc	Balanced	H-D

Heads brand	H-D ported-flowed	Cam brand	Sifton

Carb brand	Weber 40mm	Cam covers	H-D

Air cleaner	SU stacks modified, K & N filter

Exhaust pipes brand	Home-made, with Supertrapp end-plates

Ignition	Andrews	Primary/derby covers	H-D modified

TRANSMISSION

Speeds	5	Clutch	Foot	Modifications	Jockey Shift

Primary drive: belt or chain	Belt

Final drive: belt or chain	Chain

BODYWORK · ACCESSORIES · PAINT

Fender brand	None		

Custom body fabrication	Danny Franssen

Petrol tank brand	Sportster, extended & lowered

Seat brand/builder	Danny Franssen	Lights	Headwinds

Paint colour	Satin allu grey	Painter's name	Alain Gielen

Graphics	Satin yellow, with white striping	Chroming	Lemmens

180

OWNER	Kenth Arvidsson, Sweden		MODEL	H-D

BIKE NAME	Red Viking		BUILDER	Kenth Arvidsson

FRAME

Frame brand	Hogtech

Stock or modified	Stretched 2½", raked 49°, chopped 1½"

Fork brand	Tolle, lengthened 23"

Swing-arm brand	Hardtail	Shocks	None

Front/Rear brake(s) brand	ISR		

Wheels brand	Home-made	Size F/R	2.75 x 18" 1.85 x 14"

Tyres size F/R	2.75 x 18" 185/14	Spokes size F/R	120/120

ENGINE

Year	1991		

Model	Evo		

Cases brand	H-D	Cylinders brand	H-D

Cubic capacity	1340 cc	Balanced	No

Heads brand	C.S.S.		

Carb brand	S & S		

Air cleaner	S & S		

Cam brand	Andrews	Cam model	E

Exhaust pipes and silencers brand	Home-made

TRANSMISSION

Speeds	4	Clutch	H-D	Modifications	H-D

Primary drive: belt or chain	1½" belt

Final drive: belt or chain	Chain, sprockets 27/46

BODYWORK · ACCESSORIES · PAINT

Fender brand (front & rear)	Front: none; Rear: home-made

Custom body fabrication	Kenth Arvidsson

Petrol tank brand	Modified Mustang

Seat brand/builder	Kenth Arvidsson	Bars	Kent

Paint colour	Black Cherry	Painter's name	Bosse Jensen

Graphics	Viking murals	Chroming	Nicroma

181

OWNER	Marié Rashussen, Sweden	MODEL	H-D

BIKE NAME	Medusa	BUILDER	Peter Jeluemyr, Balls Choppers

FRAME

Frame brand	H-D '55		
Stock or modified	H-D stretched 1", raked 44°		
Fork brand	Tolle, modified		
Swing-arm brand	Hardtail	Shocks	None
Front/Rear brake(s) brand	Tolle ISR		
Wheels brand	Akront rim, home-made hub	Size F/R	19" 19"
Tyres brand	Pirelli ZR 17	Size F/R	90/90/19 180/55/19

ENGINE

Year	1993		
Model	Evo		
Cases brand	H-D	Cylinders brand	H-D
Cubic capacity	1340 cc	Balanced	H-D
Heads brand	H-D		
Carb brand	H-D		
Air cleaner	H-D		
Cam brand	H-D	Cam model	H-D
Exhaust pipes and silencers brand	Home-made, stainless steel		

TRANSMISSION

Speeds	5	Clutch	H-D	Modifications	
Primary drive: belt or chain	Chain				
Final drive: belt or chain	Chain				

BODYWORK ACCESSORIES PAINT

Fender brand (front & rear)	Front: none; Rear: flat modified 2"		
Custom body fabrication	Balls Choppers		
Petrol tank brand	Yamaha 125		
Seat brand/builder	Bosse Sybo, Sweden		
Paint colour	Snake Skin	Painter's name	Ray Hill
Graphics	Medusa		

182

OWNER	DiDi/Custom Ranch	MODEL	FXST

BIKE NAME	John Deere	BUILDER	Custom Ranch

FRAME

Frame brand	Softail/VG Frames, Netherlands		
Stock or modified	Stretched 1", raked 36° & lowered 2"		
Fork brand	Springer, 2" under		
Swing-arm brand	VG Frames	Shocks	Fournaler air shocks
Front/Rear brake(s) brand	ISR, stainless steel brackets		
Wheels brand	SSC	Size F/R	15" 15"
Tyres brand	Metzeler	Size F/R	150/90/15 220/70/15

ENGINE

Year	1995				
Model	Evo		Bore	$3^5/_8$	Stroke	$4^5/_8$
Cases brand	S & S		Cylinders brand	S & S	
Cubic capacity	1600 cc		Balanced	Yes, by S & S USA	
Heads brand	S & S		Cam brand	S & S 562	
Carb brand	S & S Super G	Cam specs	Lift/Dur High Performance		
Air cleaner	S & S Teardrop		Lifter blocks	S & S	
Exhaust pipes brand	Custom Ranch				
Ignition	Dynas Single Fire	Primary/derby covers	3" Zellner belt		

TRANSMISSION

Speeds	4	Clutch	Zellner, Germany	Modifications	Andrews Gears
Primary drive: belt or chain	Zellner belt, Germany				
Final drive: belt or chain	SSC chain, sprockets 24/49				

BODYWORK ACCESSORIES PAINT

Fender brand (front & rear)	Custom Ranch by Gabor				
Custom body fabrication	Frame moulded by Smith				
Petrol tank brand	Custom Ranch 6 Gal.	Bars	Custom Ranch 118cm		
Seat brand/builder	Custom Ranch	Lights	Oldstyle		
Paint colour	John Deere Colours	Painter's name	Hartl's Car & Bike		
Graphics	Gabor	Chroming	All cast iron parts		

183

140

Daytona USA
IMPORT · EXPORT, INC.
CLASSIC & EXOTIC CARS & MOTORCYCLES

517

185 186 187

190 191

142

188

189

192

193

194

195

205

206

207

208

209

210

146

211

212

213

147

Glossary

1. Bikes

ACCEL
Aftermarket ignition component manufacturers.

AERMACCHI
An Italian motorcycle manufacturing company of which Harley acquired a half share in 1960 as a way to produce small capacity lightweight motorcycles. The Japanese dominate this market and in 1977 Harley sold its share back to the Italians.

AMF
American Machine & Foundry, an industrial conglomerate who acquired Harley-Davidson in 1969 but sold it to the management in 1980.

APEHANGERS
Tall handlebars, so named because of the riding position with outstretched arms they dictate.

BAY AREA
San Francisco's Bay Area which has spawned its own styles of custom Harleys.

BIG TWIN
The term used to describe the large capacity Harley V-twins to differentiate them from the smaller capacity Sportster models.

BILLET
The term used to describe custom motorcycle parts machined from billet aluminium on CNC machines.

BLOCKHEAD
An American nickname for the current Harley-Davidson Evolution engine.

BLOWER
Slang term for a Supercharger.

BOBBER
One of the basic stripped Harleys and Indians from which choppers evolved.

BUELL
A sportsbike-styled motorcycle designed around a Sportster engine by Eric Buell and now marketed by Harley-Davidson.

CHOPPER
A bike cut down or customised to a specific style of motorcycle, often a Harley-Davidson.

CHROME SPECIALTIES INC
A large American independent aftermarket manufacturer and supplier of custom motorcycle parts.

COFFIN TANK
A once-popular custom petrol tank, so described because it was shaped like a small coffin.

CUSTOM CHROME INC
A large American independent aftermarket manufacturer and supplier of custom motorcycle parts.

DRAG PIPES
Dragstrip-inspired exhaust pipes.

DRAG SPECIALTIES
A large American independent aftermarket manufacturer and supplier of custom motorcycle parts.

FLATHEAD

American slang term for a side-valve engine regardless of manufacturer.

FRISCO-STYLE

When the petrol tank is mounted high on the frame top tube it is described as 'Frisco-style' because the fashion originated in San Fransisco.

225

FX

The designation given to the Super Glide models; the F indicated they were 74 cubic inch machines, while the X indicated the use of the Sportster front end.

FXR

Harley's designation for the rubber-mounted engine FX models.

GARBAGE WAGON

Derogatory slang term for a dresser.

226

GIRDER FORK

A particular type of motorcycle fork that lends itself to chopper usage because of its clean lines and ease of fabrication.

HARDTAIL

Slang term for a rigid-framed motor-cycle (i.e. with no rear suspension).

227

MODEL V
The Big Twin flathead V-twin produced by Harley-Davidson between 1930 and 1937.

MUSTANG TANK
A popular petrol tank used by custom bike builders and originally sourced from American Mustang mopeds although now manufactured specifically for custom bikes.

NEMPCO
A large American independent aftermarket manufacturer and supplier of custom motorcycle parts.

PANHEAD
The slang term for the overhead valve V-twin engines manufactured by Harley-Davidson between 1948 and 1965. They are so described because the rocker covers look like upturned cooking pans.

PERFORMANCE MACHINE
A noted aftermarket braking components manufacturer.

P-PAD
A pillion-pad rear seat.

PRISM TANK
An angular type of custom petrol tank that appeared faceted and was popular particularly in the '70s.

PRO-STREET
A contemporary style of custom Harley that takes its name and style from a particular class of drag race bike.

RAKE AND TRAIL
The dimensions of a motorcycle's frame and forks that determine the handling characteristics.

RIGID
A type of motorcycle frame without rear suspension as made by Harley-Davidson until 1958.

RIKUO
Harley-Davidsons briefly produced under licence in Japan before World War Two.

RISERS
The brackets that clamp the handlebars to the top of the forks. Taller risers lift the handlebars higher.

RUB
A slightly derogatory term for the 'Rich Urban Bikers' who flocked into Harley ownership when it became fashionable during the '80s.

S & S
Smith & Smith; a noted aftermarket performance engine components manufacturer.

SERVICAR
A three-wheeled utility machine manufactured by Harley-Davidson between 1932 and 1973 that became the basis for many custom trikes.

SHOTGUN PIPES
A custom style of exhaust where the shape of the silencer resembles that of a pump-action shotgun.

SHOVELHEAD
The slang term for the overhead valve V-twin engines manufactured by Harley-Davidson between 1966 and 1984. They are so described because the rocker covers look like the backs of upturned shovels.

SISSY BAR
A rear-mounted bar that acts as a backrest but often doubles as a rear fender strut and licence plate mount.

SOFTAIL
A type of frame currently manufactured by Harley-Davidson that appears rigid but has hidden rear suspension.

SOLO SEAT
The small single seat initially fitted to Sportsters which became popular for use on choppers.

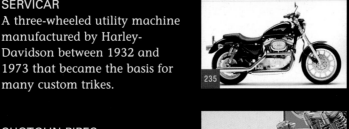

SPORTSTER
A smaller capacity Harley-Davidson in production from 1957 to present. They were initially introduced to compete with the imported British bikes.

SPORTSTER TANK
The graceful petrol tank from a Sportster is a popular choice for custom builders to use on other models.

SPRINGER FORK
An early type of sprung motorcycle fork used by Harley-Davidson until 1949 and reintroduced in the '80s on nostalgic models.

STRAIGHTLEG FRAME
The 1955–1957 rigid Harley frame sought after by custom builders because of its clean lines. It is known as a straightleg because the front downtubes are straight.

STRETCH
The longitudinal extension of a Harley frame.

SWING-ARM
The pivoting rear part of a motorcycle frame that provides rear suspension.

TELESCOPIC FORKS
Hydraulic telescopic forks introduced on Harleys with the Hydra-Glide of 1949.

238

V-TWIN
The term used to describe a two-cylinder motorcycle engine with the cylinders arranged in a V configuration.

239

V-TWIN MANUFACTURING
A large American independent aftermarket manufacturer and supplier of custom motorcycle parts.

W&W CYCLES
A large European independent aftermarket manufacturer and supplier of custom motorcycle parts.

WISHBONE FRAME

WL
The Harley-Davidson designation for the 45 cubic inch displacement sidevalve V-twins made between 1937 and 1951.

XA
An experimental flat twin Harley-Davidson built in limited numbers at the request of the US Army during World War Two.

240

XA SPRINGERS
Springer forks from the XA model became popular for bobbers and choppers because they were longer than those used on other Harleys of the time.

241

XL
The factory's designation for Sportster models.

XR
The designation given to machines such as the racing XR-750; the X indicated Sportster while the R signified

Glossary

2. Bikers

ABATE
A Brotherhood Against Totalitarian Enactments. US-based riders' rights pressure group.

AMA
American Motorcycle Association. The organisation which coined the '1%' label (see *Hollister* entry).

AWOL
UK-based European custom bike and lifestyle magazine.

BACK STREET HEROES
UK-based European custom bike magazine.

BANDIDOS MC
A 1% motorcycle club founded in Texas and now worldwide.

BARGER, RALPH 'SONNY'
One of the founders of the Oakland chapter of the HAMC.

BATTISTINIS CUSTOM CYCLES
Custom bike builder and parts distributor based in Bournemouth, England.

BEETLES MC
The fictional motorcycle club led by Lee Marvin in *The Wild One*.

BILLY
The character played by Dennis Hopper in *Easy Rider*.

BLACK REBELS MC
The fictional motorcycle club led by Marlon Brando in *The Wild One*.

BLUE ANGELS MC
Long-standing and large Scottish 1% motorcycle club.

BMF
British Motorcyclists' Federation, the UK equivalent of the AMA.

BULLDOG BASH
The Annual Biker Party run (since 1987) at the dragstrip outside Stratford-upon-Avon, organised by HAMC England.

COBRA MOTORCYCLE ENGINEERING
John Parry's renowned British custom frame manufacturer.

COLOURS
The embroidered badges of the 1% motorcycle clubs.

CUSTOM CHOPPER COOKBOOK

A softback manual written by Mike Geokan that details the hardcore nuts and bolts of building custom Harleys.

DAVIDSON, WILLIE G.

Grandson of founder William A. Davidson who joined Harley-Davidson's design department in 1963. He later designed the Super Glide and XLCR models.

DAYTONA, FLORIDA

Home of the annual Daytona 200, a 200-mile race around which the famous Bikeweek revolves.

EASY RIDER

The 1969 film starring Peter Fonda and Dennis Hopper that follows the two characters on the road to Mardi Gras aboard Panhead choppers.

EASYRIDERS

American magazine dedicated to custom Harley-Davidsons.

ELECTRA GLIDE IN BLUE

A 1973 film based around a motorcycle cop.

EUROPEAN DEALER NEWS

UK-based Harley and custom parts trade magazine.

FEM

Federation of European Motorcyclists. European riders' rights pressure group.

FINKS MC

Long-standing and large Australian 1% motorcycle club.

FREEWAY

France-based European custom bike magazine.

FREEWHEELS

A large annual French bike show and biker party near Clermont Ferrand hosted by HAMC France.

FREEWHEELERS MC

Independent Irish 1% motorcycle club.

HAMC

Hells Angels Motorcycle Club. A 1% motorcycle club founded in California and now worldwide.

HAMSTERS MC

An American motorcycle club dedicated to building and riding custom Harleys.

HARLEY-DAVIDSON 45 CLUB

UK-based club for owners of sidevalve 45 cubic inch Harley-Davidsons.

HARLEY-DAVIDSON RIDERS CLUB OF GREAT BRITAIN

Independent Harley club founded in the UK in 1949.

HARLEY OWNERS GROUP (HOG)
Factory-backed and run Harley riders' organisation worldwide.

HARRIS, DR MAZ
British Hells Angel and author of *Bikers; Birth of a modern day outlaw*, published by Faber and Faber in 1985.

HEAVY DUTY
UK-based European custom bike magazine.

HELLS ANGELS MC
A 1% motorcycle club founded in California and now world-wide.

HELLS ANGELS MC ENGLAND
The English 1% motorcycle club is an official part of the world-wide brotherhood of Hells Angels and one of the three largest 1% clubs in this country.

HIGH PERFORMANCE
Germany-based European custom bike magazine.

HOLLISTER, CALIFORNIA
The AMA races in this town in 1947 became a little rowdy and led to a few arrests, causing the AMA to distance itself from the 1% of disreputable motor-cyclists.

IRON HORSE
American magazine dedicated to choppers.

KENT CUSTOM BIKE SHOW
The oldest annual custom bike show in Europe, founded in 1979 by Hells Angels MC, Kent, England.

KNIEVEL, EVIL
American stunt rider who made numerous motorcycle jumps aboard an XR-750 Harley.

LACONIA, NEW HAMPSHIRE
The venue for the large annual bike rally around the Loudon race.

LEON, RAY
Ray Leon, along with John Wallace, was among the very first in Britain to chop Harleys using the then plentiful war surplus WLA and WLC '45s in the early 1970s.

THE LOVELESS
Kathryn Bigelow's cult 1981 film about a group of riders en route to Daytona, Florida during the '50s.

256

LYNCH REPORT
A 1965 California law enforcement agency report about 1% motorcycle clubs. It was widely circulated and reported although based largely on supposition.

MACDONALD, W. N.
Author of 'Outlaw Motorcycle Gangs', a not wholly factual report published by the *Royal Canadian Mounted Police Gazette* in 1994.

MAG
Motorcycle Action Group. UK riders' rights pressure group.

MASK
A film based on the true story of Rocky Dennis starring Cher and Sam Elliott that showed a 1% MC in a favourable light.

MC
Motorcycle club.

MACDONALD, W. N.
Author of 'Outlaw Motorcycle Gangs', a not wholly factual report published by the *Royal Canadian Mounted Police Gazette* in 1994.

MILWAUKEE, WISCONSIN
The American city where the Harley-Davidson factory is based.

257

NCC
National Chopper Club, a club dedicated to building and riding custom bikes founded in Britain in 1973 that now has constituent clubs all over Europe.

258

NESS, ARLEN
Noted and long-standing San Francisco Bay Area custom bike builder.

259

NICHOLSON, JACK
Actor who starred with Fonda and Hopper in *Easy Rider* but also earlier in *Hell's Angels On Wheels*, one of a series of biker exploitation movies that included *Hell's Angels '69*, *The Rebel Rousers* and *The Wild Angels*.

NOTTINGHAM CUSTOM CYCLES
An English custom bike fabricator based in the city of Nottingham.

ONE PERCENTER
A member of a 1% MC (see *Hollister* entry).

OUTLAWS MC (ENGLAND)
Independent English 1% motorcycle club, one of the three largest in this country.

OUTLAWS MC (USA)
Long-standing and large 1% motorcycle club, now worldwide.

PATCH
Slang term for 1% colours.

PEREWITZ, DAVE
Noted US custom builder based in Brockton, Massachusetts.

A PLACE IN HELL
Allegedly the biography of one of the first Hells Angels by H. R. Kaye, published in 1968.

PLANET ENGINEERING
A custom bike shop based in Wiltshire, England.

QUADROPHENIA
A 1979 British film based on the mods and rockers conflict of the '60s.

RAT'S HOLE SHOW
A noted custom bike show held annually during Bikeweek in Daytona, Florida and more latterly in Sturgis during the Black Hills Classic.

REBELS MC
Long-standing and large Australian 1% motorcycle club.

REED, JOHN
English custom bike builder who came to prominence in the '70s with Triumph and Yamaha custom bikes and who now designs parts for Californian Custom Chrome Inc.

REYNOLDS, FRANK
Along with M. McClure, wrote the autobiographical *Freewheelin' Frank* about the early days of Hells Angels MC, published by Grove Press Inc in 1967.

ROCK & BLUES
A big annual custom bike show and biker party organised by the Derbyshire chapter of the Outlaws MC.

SATAN'S SLAVES MC
Independent English 1% motorcycle club, one of the three largest in this country.

SMITH, DONNIE
A noted US custom bike builder based in Minneapolis.

SONS OF SILENCE MC
Long-standing and large
American 1% motorcycle club.

STURGIS, SOUTH DAKOTA
The small town that is host to
the annual Black Hills Rally
founded by Pappy Hoel and the
Jackpine Gipsies MC in the '30s.

STURGIS
A limited edition Harley-
Davidson Super Glide
introduced in 1980.

SUPER RALLY
Annual rally for Harley-
Davidson owners held in a
different European country each
year and organised by the local
Harley Riders Club.

THOMPSON, HUNTER S.
Author of the 1966 book *Hell's
Angels*, one of the first serious
books about the 1%.

THUNDER CYCLES
Germany-based European
custom bike magazine.

VQ
An upmarket American custom
Harley magazine from the
publishers of *Easyriders*.

WARR, F. H
Europe's oldest Harley-Davidson
dealership, established in 1926
and noted contributor to the
British Harley-Davidson scene,
for the past 75 years.

A WAYWARD ANGEL
George Wethern and Vincent
Colnett's 1978 account of riding
with the Hells Angels, co-
authored by a former member.

THE WILD ONE
A 1954 film made by Stanley
Kramer fictionalising the
goings-on at Hollister in July
1947.

WOLF, DANIEL R.
Author of *The Rebels: a brotherhood of outlaw bikers*, a socio-
logical study of a Canadian 1%
club published by the University
of Toronto Press in 1991.

WYATT
The Captain America character
played by Peter Fonda in *Easy
Rider*.

YORK, PENNSYLVANIA
The American city where a
Harley-Davidson plant is based.

Glossaries compiled by
John Carroll

163

Index

Barbican Art Gallery would like to thank the following individuals and collections for the loan of photographs for use in this publication:

Kenth Arvidsson, *97, 112, 181*
AWOL, 243
Back Street Heroes, 101
Conrad Bodman, *124, 132, 137*
British Film Institute, Stills, Posters and Designs, *77, 89, 256*
British Film Institute, Stills, Posters and Designs/Columbia
     Pictures, *78, 79, 91, 92, 93, 234, 245, 248, 266, 267*
George Barris Collection, *19–21*
Nicolas Chauvin, *116, 117, 179*
Bigmachines/Steve Coonan, *65*
Bal Croce, *76, 81–90, 259*
Drag Specialties, *163, 165*
Bob Dron, *2, 47–49*
Easyriders, 100
Flicks, *80, 86*
Danny Franssen, *95, 103, 180*
Freeway, 249
Andrew Haines, *18, 42, 118*
Heavy Duty, 246, 251, 252
High Performance, 254
Cyril Huze, *74, 164*
Harley-Davidson Motor Company Archives, *15, 16, 39, 41, 56,
122, 125–129, 148, 149, 171, 221–223, 230, 233, 235,
     237, 238, 240, 241*

Geoff Kaine, *94, 173, 228*
Ian Mutch, *98, 99, 106, 232*
Mazda, *43*
Arlen Ness, *72*
Ted Polhemus, *12–14, 17, 23–26, 31, 33, 37, 38, 107, 145,
     257*
Marié Rashussen, *111, 182*
Dieter Rebman, *54, 96, 139, 231*
Garry Stuart, *1, 3–7, 9–10, 27–30, 32, 34–36, 40, 45, 51, 52,
     55, 57, 58, 68, 75, 104, 105, 119, 120, 130, 131, 133, 136,
     138, 140–144, 147, 150–153, 176–178, 184–215, 218, 219,
224–227, 229, 236, 239, 242, 247, 250, 253, 258, 260,
     262–264*
Gerd Scheidel, *113–115, 123, 183*
Tim Remus, *8, 46, 50, 53, 59–64, 69–71, 73, 75, 135, 146,
     156–161, 164, 166, 167, 170, 220, 261*
San Francisco Chronicle, 255
Alain Sauquet, *109, 174*
Richard Taylor, *44, 102, 134, 175, 216, 217*
Steve Terry, *66, 67, 168, 169*
VQ, 265
Matthew Ward, *11*
John Warr, *154*
Karl Wilson, *108, 110, 172, 244*
Sid Wellings, *121*
Zweirad-Museum, Neckarslum, Germany, *155*

Every effort has been made to identify the photographers and owners of reproduction rights. Barbican Art Gallery will be happy to rectify any inaccuracies in further editions.